50 Classic British Pub Recipes for Home

By: Kelly Johnson

Table of Contents

- Fish and Chips
- Shepherd's Pie
- Steak and Ale Pie
- Bangers and Mash
- Ploughman's Lunch
- Full English Breakfast
- Beef Wellington
- Toad in the Hole
- Scotch Eggs
- Cornish Pasty
- Lancashire Hotpot
- Welsh Rarebit
- Beef Stew and Dumplings
- Chicken Tikka Masala
- Pork Pie
- Bubble and Squeak
- Pork Scratchings
- Mushy Peas
- Sausage Rolls
- Liver and Onions
- Black Pudding
- Scotch Broth
- Pea and Ham Soup
- Steak and Kidney Pie
- Spotted Dick
- Sticky Toffee Pudding
- Eton Mess
- Trifle
- Apple Crumble
- Bread and Butter Pudding
- Roast Beef with Yorkshire Pudding
- Chicken and Leek Pie

- Chicken Curry
- Gammon Steak with Pineapple
- Beef and Ale Stew
- Fish Pie
- Smoked Haddock and Poached Eggs
- Beef Bourguignon
- Chicken and Mushroom Pie
- Jacket Potato with Various Toppings
- Cheese and Onion Pie
- Cheese Platter with Pickles
- Plaice with Tartar Sauce
- Mince and Onion Pie
- Chicken Liver Pâté
- Salmon Fishcakes
- Vegetable Soup
- Welsh Cawl
- Beef and Guinness Stew
- Rarebit Muffins

Fish and Chips

Ingredients:

For the fish:

- 4 fillets of white fish (such as cod, haddock, or pollock)
- 1 cup all-purpose flour
- 1 teaspoon baking powder
- 1 teaspoon salt
- 1 cup cold water
- Vegetable oil for frying

For the chips:

- 4 large potatoes, peeled and cut into thick strips
- Salt, to taste

For serving:

- Malt vinegar
- Tartar sauce
- Lemon wedges

Instructions:

Start by preparing the chips. Rinse the potato strips under cold water to remove excess starch. Pat them dry with a clean kitchen towel.
Heat vegetable oil in a deep fryer or large pot to 350°F (175°C).
Carefully add the potato strips to the hot oil, in batches if necessary to avoid overcrowding the fryer. Fry for about 5-6 minutes or until the chips are golden

brown and crispy. Remove them from the oil using a slotted spoon and place them on a plate lined with paper towels to drain excess oil. Sprinkle with salt while still hot.

In a mixing bowl, whisk together the flour, baking powder, and salt. Slowly add the cold water, whisking continuously, until you have a smooth batter with the consistency of heavy cream.

Pat the fish fillets dry with paper towels. Season them lightly with salt.

Dip each fish fillet into the batter, making sure it is fully coated.

Carefully place the battered fish into the hot oil. Fry for about 5-7 minutes, turning occasionally, until the fish is golden brown and cooked through. The cooking time will depend on the thickness of the fillets.

Once cooked, remove the fish from the oil and place them on a plate lined with paper towels to drain any excess oil.

Serve the fish and chips hot, with malt vinegar, tartar sauce, and lemon wedges on the side.

Enjoy your homemade Fish and Chips, a classic British pub favorite!

Shepherd's Pie

Ingredients:

For the filling:

- 1 lb (450g) ground lamb or beef
- 1 onion, finely chopped
- 2 carrots, diced
- 2 cloves garlic, minced
- 1 tablespoon tomato paste
- 1 tablespoon Worcestershire sauce
- 1 cup beef or vegetable broth
- 1 cup frozen peas
- Salt and pepper, to taste
- 2 tablespoons olive oil

For the mashed potato topping:

- 2 lbs (about 1 kg) potatoes, peeled and cut into chunks
- 4 tablespoons butter
- 1/4 cup milk or cream
- Salt and pepper, to taste

Instructions:

Preheat your oven to 375°F (190°C).

Start by making the mashed potato topping. Place the potato chunks in a large pot of salted water. Bring to a boil and cook until the potatoes are fork-tender, about 15-20 minutes.

Drain the potatoes and return them to the pot. Add the butter, milk or cream, salt, and pepper. Mash the potatoes until smooth and creamy. Set aside.

In a large skillet or frying pan, heat the olive oil over medium heat. Add the chopped onion and diced carrots. Cook until softened, about 5 minutes.

Add the minced garlic to the pan and cook for an additional minute until fragrant. Increase the heat to medium-high and add the ground lamb or beef to the skillet. Cook, breaking up the meat with a spoon, until browned and cooked through, about 5-7 minutes.

Stir in the tomato paste and Worcestershire sauce, coating the meat and vegetables evenly.

Pour in the beef or vegetable broth and bring the mixture to a simmer. Allow it to cook for a few minutes until the liquid has reduced slightly.

Stir in the frozen peas and season the filling with salt and pepper to taste. Remove the skillet from the heat.

Transfer the meat mixture to a baking dish and spread it out evenly.

Spoon the mashed potatoes over the top of the meat mixture, spreading them out with a spatula to cover the entire surface.

Use a fork to create a decorative pattern on the surface of the mashed potatoes. Place the baking dish in the preheated oven and bake for 25-30 minutes, or until the mashed potatoes are golden brown and the filling is bubbling.

Remove the Shepherd's Pie from the oven and let it cool for a few minutes before serving.

Serve hot, and enjoy this classic British comfort dish!

Feel free to adjust the seasonings and ingredients according to your taste preferences.

Steak and Ale Pie

Ingredients:

For the filling:

- 1.5 lbs (680g) beef steak, cut into bite-sized pieces (such as sirloin or chuck)
- 2 tablespoons all-purpose flour
- Salt and pepper, to taste
- 2 tablespoons vegetable oil
- 1 onion, chopped
- 2 cloves garlic, minced
- 2 carrots, diced
- 2 celery stalks, diced
- 1 cup (240ml) ale or stout
- 1 cup (240ml) beef broth
- 2 tablespoons tomato paste
- 1 tablespoon Worcestershire sauce
- 2 bay leaves
- 1 teaspoon dried thyme
- 1 teaspoon dried rosemary
- 1 teaspoon paprika
- 1 tablespoon cornstarch (optional, for thickening)

For the pastry:

- 1 sheet of store-bought puff pastry, thawed if frozen
- 1 egg, beaten (for egg wash)

Instructions:

Preheat your oven to 375°F (190°C).
In a large bowl, season the beef pieces with salt and pepper, then toss them in the flour until coated.
Heat the vegetable oil in a large skillet or Dutch oven over medium-high heat. Add the floured beef pieces in batches and cook until browned on all sides. Remove the beef from the skillet and set aside.
In the same skillet, add the chopped onion, minced garlic, diced carrots, and diced celery. Cook until the vegetables are softened, about 5 minutes.
Return the browned beef to the skillet. Pour in the ale or stout, beef broth, and add the tomato paste, Worcestershire sauce, bay leaves, dried thyme, dried rosemary, and paprika. Stir well to combine.
Bring the mixture to a simmer, then cover and cook over low heat for about 1.5 to 2 hours, or until the beef is tender. If the mixture is too thin, you can thicken it by mixing cornstarch with a little water and stirring it into the filling. Allow it to simmer for a few more minutes until thickened.
While the filling is simmering, roll out the puff pastry on a lightly floured surface to fit the top of your pie dish.
Once the filling is ready, remove the bay leaves and spoon it into a pie dish.
Place the rolled-out puff pastry over the top of the pie dish, trimming any excess pastry around the edges. Use a fork to press down the edges of the pastry to seal them to the dish.
Brush the beaten egg over the pastry to create a golden finish.
Cut a few slits in the pastry to allow steam to escape during baking.
Place the pie dish on a baking sheet (to catch any drips) and bake in the preheated oven for 30-35 minutes, or until the pastry is golden brown and crispy.
Once baked, remove the pie from the oven and let it cool for a few minutes before serving.
Serve hot slices of Steak and Ale Pie with your favorite sides, such as mashed potatoes and peas.

Enjoy this hearty and flavorful British classic!

Bangers and Mash

Ingredients:

For the bangers:

- 6-8 pork sausages (traditional British bangers if available)
- 1 tablespoon vegetable oil

For the mashed potatoes:

- 2 lbs (about 1 kg) potatoes, peeled and cut into chunks
- 4 tablespoons butter
- 1/4 cup milk or cream
- Salt and pepper, to taste

For the onion gravy:

- 2 onions, thinly sliced
- 2 tablespoons butter or vegetable oil
- 2 tablespoons all-purpose flour
- 2 cups (480ml) beef or chicken broth
- Salt and pepper, to taste

Instructions:

Start by preparing the mashed potatoes. Place the potato chunks in a large pot of salted water. Bring to a boil and cook until the potatoes are fork-tender, about 15-20 minutes.

While the potatoes are cooking, you can start preparing the onion gravy. In a skillet or saucepan, melt the butter or heat the vegetable oil over medium heat. Add the thinly sliced onions and cook, stirring occasionally, until they are soft and caramelized, about 15-20 minutes.

Once the onions are caramelized, sprinkle the flour over them and stir to coat evenly. Cook for another minute to cook off the raw flour taste.

Gradually pour in the beef or chicken broth, stirring constantly to prevent lumps from forming. Bring the mixture to a simmer and cook until the gravy has thickened, about 5-7 minutes. Season with salt and pepper to taste. Keep the gravy warm over low heat while you prepare the rest of the dish.

When the potatoes are cooked, drain them and return them to the pot. Add the butter, milk or cream, salt, and pepper. Mash the potatoes until smooth and creamy. Adjust the consistency with more milk or cream if needed. Cover the pot to keep the mashed potatoes warm.

In a separate skillet, heat the vegetable oil over medium-high heat. Add the sausages and cook, turning occasionally, until they are browned and cooked through, about 12-15 minutes.

Once everything is ready, serve the bangers and mash on plates, with a generous serving of mashed potatoes, sausages, and onion gravy.

Optionally, you can serve with steamed green vegetables such as peas or broccoli on the side.

Enjoy your homemade Bangers and Mash, a classic British comfort food dish!

Feel free to customize this recipe by using different types of sausages or adding herbs and spices to the mashed potatoes for extra flavor.

Ploughman's Lunch

Ingredients:

- Slices of crusty bread or a bread roll
- Assorted cheeses (such as cheddar, Stilton, or Red Leicester)
- Pickles or chutney (such as Branston pickle or piccalilli)
- Sliced ham or roast beef
- Hard-boiled eggs, halved
- Cherry tomatoes or slices of cucumber
- Mixed salad leaves
- Butter, for spreading (optional)

Instructions:

Start by arranging a selection of cheeses on a serving platter or board. You can include a variety of cheeses, such as cheddar, Stilton, or Red Leicester, and slice them into bite-sized pieces.

Next, add slices of crusty bread or a bread roll to the platter. If desired, you can lightly toast the bread beforehand.

Place pickles or chutney, such as Branston pickle or piccalilli, in small bowls or jars and place them on the platter alongside the cheeses and bread.

Add slices of ham or roast beef to the platter, arranging them neatly next to the cheeses and bread.

Arrange halved hard-boiled eggs, cherry tomatoes, or slices of cucumber on the platter for added variety and color.

Scatter mixed salad leaves around the platter to add freshness and texture to the meal.

Optionally, provide butter for spreading on the bread.

Serve the Ploughman's Lunch immediately, allowing diners to assemble their own plates with a selection of the ingredients provided.

Enjoy this simple and satisfying meal, perfect for a leisurely lunch or a picnic!

Ploughman's Lunch is highly customizable, so feel free to add or substitute ingredients based on your preferences and what's available. Additionally, you can serve it with a pint of beer or cider for an authentic British pub experience.

Full English Breakfast

Ingredients:

- Bacon rashers (back bacon or streaky bacon)
- Pork sausages
- Black pudding (a type of blood sausage)
- Eggs (fried, poached, or scrambled)
- Baked beans
- Grilled tomatoes
- Sautéed mushrooms
- Toast or fried bread
- Butter, for spreading

- Optional extras: hash browns, fried potatoes, bubble and squeak (a dish made from leftover vegetables and potatoes), fried onions, and HP sauce or ketchup for serving

Instructions:

Start by cooking the bacon rashers and pork sausages. You can grill, fry, or bake them according to your preference until they are cooked through and golden brown.

While the bacon and sausages are cooking, prepare the black pudding. Depending on the type you have, you may need to slice it and fry or grill it until heated through and crispy on the outside.

Cook the eggs to your liking. You can fry them sunny-side up or over-easy, poach them, or scramble them. Season with salt and pepper if desired.

Heat the baked beans in a saucepan or microwave until hot.

Grill or broil the tomatoes until they are slightly charred and softened.

Sauté the mushrooms in a little butter or oil until they are tender and golden brown.

Toast slices of bread or fry bread in a little butter until golden brown and crisp.

Once all the components are cooked, assemble the Full English Breakfast on a large plate or serving platter. Arrange the bacon, sausages, black pudding, eggs, grilled tomatoes, sautéed mushrooms, and baked beans on the plate.

Serve the breakfast with toast or fried bread on the side, along with butter for spreading.

Optionally, you can add extras such as hash browns, fried potatoes, bubble and squeak, or fried onions to the plate.

Serve the Full English Breakfast hot, accompanied by HP sauce or ketchup for those who like a bit of extra flavor.

Enjoy this hearty and satisfying breakfast, perfect for starting the day off right!

Feel free to adjust the components of the Full English Breakfast according to your preferences and dietary restrictions. It's a versatile meal that can be customized to suit individual tastes.

Beef Wellington

Ingredients:

- 1 ½ to 2 lbs (680 to 900g) beef tenderloin, trimmed and tied
- Salt and black pepper, to taste
- 2 tablespoons olive oil
- 2 tablespoons Dijon mustard
- 8 oz (225g) pâté (such as fois gras or mushroom duxelles)
- 1 sheet of puff pastry, thawed if frozen

- Flour, for dusting
- 1 egg, beaten (for egg wash)

Instructions:

Preheat your oven to 425°F (220°C).
Season the beef tenderloin generously with salt and black pepper.
Heat the olive oil in a large skillet over high heat. Sear the beef on all sides until browned, about 2 minutes per side. Remove from heat and let it cool slightly.
Once the beef has cooled, brush the entire surface with Dijon mustard.
Roll out the puff pastry on a lightly floured surface to a size large enough to completely wrap the beef.
Spread the pâté evenly over the top of the beef tenderloin.
Place the beef in the center of the puff pastry sheet. Fold the pastry over the beef, sealing the edges tightly. Trim any excess pastry if necessary.
Place the wrapped beef seam side down on a baking sheet lined with parchment paper.
Brush the entire surface of the puff pastry with beaten egg to create a golden finish.
Use a sharp knife to score the surface of the pastry lightly, being careful not to cut all the way through.
Bake the Beef Wellington in the preheated oven for 35-40 minutes, or until the pastry is golden brown and the beef reaches your desired level of doneness. For medium-rare, aim for an internal temperature of 130-135°F (55-57°C) when measured with a meat thermometer.
Once baked, remove the Beef Wellington from the oven and let it rest for 10 minutes before slicing.
Slice the Beef Wellington into thick portions and serve hot, accompanied by your favorite sides such as mashed potatoes and roasted vegetables.
Enjoy this elegant and flavorful dish with your family and friends!

Beef Wellington is a show-stopping dish that's perfect for special occasions or dinner parties. It requires a bit of effort but the result is well worth it!

Toad in the Hole

Ingredients:

- 8-10 pork sausages
- 2 tablespoons vegetable oil

- 1 cup (240ml) all-purpose flour
- 1 cup (240ml) milk
- 2 large eggs
- Salt and pepper, to taste
- Optional: onion gravy for serving

Instructions:

Preheat your oven to 425°F (220°C).

Place the sausages in a large baking dish or roasting pan. Drizzle with vegetable oil, tossing to coat the sausages evenly. Make sure they are spaced out in the dish.

Place the baking dish in the preheated oven and cook the sausages for 10 minutes. This will partially cook them and start to render some of the fat.

While the sausages are cooking, prepare the Yorkshire pudding batter. In a mixing bowl, whisk together the flour, milk, eggs, salt, and pepper until smooth and well combined. Let the batter rest for 10-15 minutes.

After the sausages have cooked for 10 minutes, carefully pour the Yorkshire pudding batter over them in the baking dish. Make sure the sausages are still spaced out evenly.

Return the baking dish to the oven and bake for an additional 25-30 minutes, or until the Yorkshire pudding is puffed up and golden brown.

While the Toad in the Hole is baking, you can prepare the onion gravy if desired. Simply sauté sliced onions in a skillet with butter until softened and caramelized, then stir in beef or vegetable broth, a splash of Worcestershire sauce, and season with salt and pepper. Let the gravy simmer until slightly thickened.

Once baked, remove the Toad in the Hole from the oven and let it cool for a few minutes.

Serve the Toad in the Hole hot, accompanied by the onion gravy if desired.

Enjoy this comforting and delicious British dish!

Toad in the Hole is often served with mashed potatoes and vegetables on the side for a complete meal. It's a hearty and satisfying dish that's perfect for a cozy dinner.

Scotch Eggs

Ingredients:

- 6 large eggs
- 1 lb (450g) ground pork sausage meat
- 1/2 teaspoon salt
- 1/4 teaspoon black pepper
- 1/2 teaspoon dried thyme
- 1/2 teaspoon dried parsley
- 1/4 teaspoon garlic powder
- 1 cup (about 120g) all-purpose flour
- 2 eggs, beaten (for egg wash)
- 1 cup (about 120g) breadcrumbs
- Vegetable oil, for frying

Instructions:

Start by boiling the eggs. Place the eggs in a saucepan and cover them with cold water. Bring the water to a boil over medium-high heat, then reduce the heat to low and simmer for 9-10 minutes.

Once the eggs are cooked, transfer them to a bowl of ice water to cool completely. Once cooled, carefully peel the eggs and set them aside.

In a mixing bowl, combine the ground pork sausage meat with salt, black pepper, dried thyme, dried parsley, and garlic powder. Mix well until the seasonings are evenly distributed.

Divide the sausage meat mixture into 6 equal portions.

Take one portion of the sausage meat mixture and flatten it out on your palm. Place a peeled hard-boiled egg in the center and gently mold the sausage meat around the egg, ensuring it is completely covered. Repeat with the remaining eggs and sausage meat.

Set up a breading station with three shallow bowls: one with flour, one with beaten eggs, and one with breadcrumbs.

Roll each sausage-wrapped egg in flour, then dip it into the beaten eggs, and finally coat it evenly with breadcrumbs. Repeat the process for a second coat of egg wash and breadcrumbs if desired.

Heat vegetable oil in a deep fryer or large pot to 350°F (175°C).

Carefully lower the Scotch eggs into the hot oil using a slotted spoon or frying basket. Fry them in batches, if necessary, to avoid overcrowding the fryer.

Fry the Scotch eggs for about 5-6 minutes, turning occasionally, until they are golden brown and crispy.

Once cooked, remove the Scotch eggs from the oil and drain them on a plate lined with paper towels.
Let the Scotch eggs cool slightly before serving.
Serve the Scotch eggs warm or at room temperature, either as a snack or appetizer.

Enjoy these homemade Scotch eggs, with their crispy exterior and deliciously savory filling!

Cornish Pasty

Ingredients:

For the pastry:

- 2 cups (250g) all-purpose flour
- 1/2 cup (113g) unsalted butter, chilled and cubed
- Pinch of salt
- 1/4 cup (60ml) cold water

For the filling:

- 1 lb (450g) beef skirt steak or chuck steak, diced
- 1 large potato, peeled and diced
- 1 onion, finely chopped
- 1 carrot, peeled and diced
- Salt and pepper, to taste
- Optional: 1 tablespoon Worcestershire sauce or beef stock concentrate for added flavor

For assembly:

- 1 egg, beaten (for egg wash)

Instructions:

Preheat your oven to 375°F (190°C).
In a large mixing bowl, combine the flour and a pinch of salt. Add the chilled butter cubes and rub them into the flour using your fingertips until the mixture resembles coarse breadcrumbs.
Gradually add the cold water to the flour mixture, mixing with a fork or your hands until a dough forms. Be careful not to overwork the dough.
Wrap the dough in plastic wrap and refrigerate it while you prepare the filling.
In a separate bowl, combine the diced beef, diced potato, chopped onion, and diced carrot. Season with salt and pepper, and add Worcestershire sauce or beef stock concentrate if using. Mix well to combine.

On a lightly floured surface, roll out the chilled pastry dough to about 1/4 inch (6mm) thickness. Use a round cutter or a small plate to cut out circles of pastry, each about 6-8 inches (15-20cm) in diameter.

Divide the filling mixture evenly among the pastry circles, placing it on one half of each circle.

Fold the other half of the pastry over the filling to encase it, then crimp the edges firmly to seal the pasties. You can use the tines of a fork to crimp the edges or pinch and fold them together.

Place the assembled pasties on a baking sheet lined with parchment paper.

Brush the tops of the pasties with beaten egg to create a golden crust when baked.

Bake the Cornish Pasties in the preheated oven for 45-50 minutes, or until the pastry is golden brown and cooked through.

Once baked, remove the pasties from the oven and let them cool slightly before serving.

Serve the Cornish Pasties warm or at room temperature, either as a snack or a meal accompanied by your favorite sides.

Enjoy these delicious and hearty Cornish Pasties, a beloved British comfort food!

Lancashire Hotpot

Ingredients:

- 1.5 lbs (680g) lamb shoulder or stewing lamb, cut into bite-sized pieces
- 2 tablespoons vegetable oil
- 2 onions, thinly sliced
- 2 carrots, diced
- 2 celery stalks, diced
- 2 cloves garlic, minced
- 2 tablespoons all-purpose flour
- 1 tablespoon tomato paste
- 2 cups (480ml) beef or lamb broth
- 1 tablespoon Worcestershire sauce
- 1 teaspoon dried thyme
- Salt and pepper, to taste
- 4 large potatoes, peeled and thinly sliced
- 2 tablespoons melted butter, for brushing

Instructions:

Preheat your oven to 350°F (175°C).
In a large ovenproof pot or Dutch oven, heat the vegetable oil over medium heat. Add the diced lamb pieces and cook until browned on all sides. Remove the lamb from the pot and set it aside.
In the same pot, add the sliced onions, diced carrots, and diced celery. Cook until the vegetables are softened, about 5 minutes.
Add the minced garlic to the pot and cook for an additional minute until fragrant. Sprinkle the flour over the vegetables in the pot and stir to coat evenly. Cook for another minute to cook off the raw flour taste.

Return the browned lamb to the pot. Add the tomato paste, beef or lamb broth, Worcestershire sauce, dried thyme, salt, and pepper. Stir well to combine.

Bring the mixture to a simmer, then cover the pot and transfer it to the preheated oven.

Bake the Lancashire Hotpot in the oven for 1.5 to 2 hours, or until the lamb is tender and the sauce has thickened slightly.

Once the lamb is cooked, remove the pot from the oven and increase the oven temperature to 400°F (200°C).

Arrange the thinly sliced potatoes on top of the lamb mixture in the pot, overlapping them slightly. Brush the sliced potatoes with melted butter.

Return the pot to the oven and bake for an additional 30-40 minutes, or until the potatoes are golden brown and crispy on top.

Once baked, remove the Lancashire Hotpot from the oven and let it cool for a few minutes before serving.

Serve the Lancashire Hotpot hot, spooning the tender lamb and vegetables onto plates and topping them with crispy slices of potato.

Enjoy this comforting and flavorful Lancashire Hotpot, a traditional British dish perfect for a cozy meal!

Welsh Rarebit

Ingredients:

- 4 slices of bread (traditional Welsh Rarebit uses thick slices of crusty bread or toast)
- 2 tablespoons unsalted butter
- 2 tablespoons all-purpose flour
- 1 teaspoon mustard powder
- 1/2 teaspoon Worcestershire sauce
- 1/2 cup (120ml) beer or ale (traditional choices include stout or ale, but any beer will work)
- 1 cup (120g) grated sharp cheddar cheese
- Salt and pepper, to taste
- Optional: a pinch of cayenne pepper or paprika for added flavor

Instructions:

Preheat your broiler or grill.

Toast the bread slices until golden brown on both sides. You can use a toaster, toaster oven, or grill for this step. Set the toasted bread aside on a baking sheet lined with parchment paper.

In a saucepan, melt the butter over medium heat.

Once the butter is melted, whisk in the flour to form a roux. Cook the roux for 1-2 minutes, stirring constantly, until it is lightly golden brown.

Gradually whisk in the beer or ale, stirring constantly to prevent lumps from forming.

Add the mustard powder and Worcestershire sauce to the saucepan, stirring to combine.

Reduce the heat to low and gradually add the grated cheddar cheese to the sauce, stirring until the cheese is melted and the sauce is smooth and thickened.

Season the cheese sauce with salt, pepper, and a pinch of cayenne pepper or paprika, if desired, for added flavor.

Once the cheese sauce is ready, spoon it evenly over the toasted bread slices, covering them completely.

Place the baking sheet with the topped bread slices under the preheated broiler or grill. Broil or grill for 2-3 minutes, or until the cheese sauce is bubbly and lightly browned on top.

Remove the Welsh Rarebit from the broiler or grill and serve immediately, while hot.

Enjoy your homemade Welsh Rarebit as a delicious and comforting snack or light meal!

Welsh Rarebit is versatile and can be customized to suit your taste preferences. Feel free to experiment with different types of cheese, spices, or additions such as sliced tomatoes or ham.

Beef Stew and Dumplings

Ingredients for Beef Stew:

- 1.5 lbs (680g) stewing beef, cut into bite-sized pieces
- 2 tablespoons all-purpose flour
- Salt and pepper, to taste
- 2 tablespoons vegetable oil
- 2 onions, chopped
- 2 carrots, sliced
- 2 celery stalks, sliced
- 2 cloves garlic, minced
- 2 tablespoons tomato paste
- 4 cups (960ml) beef broth
- 2 bay leaves
- 1 teaspoon dried thyme
- 1 teaspoon dried rosemary
- 2 tablespoons Worcestershire sauce
- 2 tablespoons cornstarch (optional, for thickening)

Ingredients for Dumplings:

- 1 cup (125g) self-rising flour

- 1/2 teaspoon salt
- 1/2 teaspoon dried thyme
- 1/2 teaspoon dried rosemary
- 2 tablespoons butter, cold and diced
- 1/2 cup (120ml) milk

Instructions:

Preheat your oven to 325°F (160°C).

In a large bowl, season the stewing beef with salt and pepper. Add the all-purpose flour and toss the beef until evenly coated.

Heat the vegetable oil in a large ovenproof pot or Dutch oven over medium-high heat. Add the floured beef pieces in batches and cook until browned on all sides. Remove the beef from the pot and set aside.

In the same pot, add the chopped onions, sliced carrots, and sliced celery. Cook until the vegetables are softened, about 5 minutes.

Add the minced garlic to the pot and cook for an additional minute until fragrant. Stir in the tomato paste and cook for another minute.

Return the browned beef to the pot. Pour in the beef broth and add the bay leaves, dried thyme, dried rosemary, and Worcestershire sauce. Stir well to combine.

Bring the stew to a simmer, then cover the pot and transfer it to the preheated oven.

Bake the beef stew in the oven for 2 to 2.5 hours, or until the beef is tender and the flavors have melded together.

While the stew is cooking, prepare the dumplings. In a mixing bowl, combine the self-rising flour, salt, dried thyme, and dried rosemary. Add the cold, diced butter and rub it into the flour mixture until it resembles coarse crumbs.

Gradually add the milk to the flour mixture, stirring with a fork until a soft dough forms. Be careful not to overmix.

Once the stew has cooked for the specified time, remove it from the oven and increase the oven temperature to 400°F (200°C).

If desired, mix cornstarch with a little water to make a slurry and stir it into the stew to thicken the sauce.

Drop spoonfuls of the dumpling mixture onto the surface of the stew, spacing them evenly.

Return the pot to the oven and bake for an additional 20-25 minutes, or until the dumplings are golden brown and cooked through.

Once baked, remove the Beef Stew and Dumplings from the oven and let it cool for a few minutes before serving.

Serve the stew and dumplings hot, spooning the tender beef and vegetables into bowls along with the savory dumplings.

Enjoy this comforting and satisfying Beef Stew and Dumplings as a hearty meal!

Chicken Tikka Masala

Ingredients for Chicken Marinade:

- 1 lb (450g) boneless, skinless chicken breasts or thighs, cut into bite-sized pieces
- 1/2 cup (120g) plain yogurt
- 2 tablespoons lemon juice
- 2 teaspoons ground cumin
- 2 teaspoons ground coriander
- 1 teaspoon paprika
- 1 teaspoon turmeric
- 1 teaspoon garam masala
- 1/2 teaspoon ground cinnamon
- 1/2 teaspoon cayenne pepper (adjust to taste for spiciness)
- 2 cloves garlic, minced
- 1-inch piece of ginger, grated
- Salt and pepper, to taste

Ingredients for Sauce:

- 2 tablespoons vegetable oil or ghee
- 1 onion, finely chopped
- 2 cloves garlic, minced
- 1-inch piece of ginger, grated
- 1 tablespoon tomato paste
- 1 teaspoon ground cumin
- 1 teaspoon ground coriander
- 1 teaspoon paprika
- 1 teaspoon garam masala
- 1/2 teaspoon ground turmeric
- 1/2 teaspoon cayenne pepper (adjust to taste for spiciness)
- 1 can (14 oz/400g) diced tomatoes
- 1 cup (240ml) heavy cream or coconut milk
- Salt and pepper, to taste
- Fresh cilantro, chopped, for garnish (optional)

Instructions:

In a mixing bowl, combine the yogurt, lemon juice, minced garlic, grated ginger, ground cumin, ground coriander, paprika, turmeric, garam masala, ground cinnamon, cayenne pepper, salt, and pepper. Mix well to combine.

Add the chicken pieces to the marinade, making sure they are well coated. Cover the bowl and refrigerate for at least 1 hour, or preferably overnight, to allow the flavors to develop.

Preheat your grill or grill pan to medium-high heat. Thread the marinated chicken pieces onto skewers and grill for 5-6 minutes on each side, or until cooked through and slightly charred. Alternatively, you can cook the chicken in the oven at 400°F (200°C) for about 20-25 minutes, or until cooked through.

While the chicken is cooking, prepare the sauce. Heat the vegetable oil or ghee in a large skillet or saucepan over medium heat. Add the chopped onion and cook until softened and translucent, about 5 minutes.

Add the minced garlic and grated ginger to the skillet, and cook for another minute until fragrant.

Stir in the tomato paste, ground cumin, ground coriander, paprika, garam masala, ground turmeric, and cayenne pepper. Cook for another minute to toast the spices.

Add the diced tomatoes (with their juices) to the skillet, stirring to combine. Bring the mixture to a simmer and let it cook for 10-15 minutes, stirring occasionally, until the sauce has thickened slightly.

Once the sauce has thickened, stir in the heavy cream or coconut milk. Allow the sauce to simmer gently for another 5 minutes, then season with salt and pepper to taste.

Add the grilled chicken pieces to the sauce, stirring gently to coat them with the sauce. Let the chicken simmer in the sauce for a few more minutes to absorb the flavors.

Serve the Chicken Tikka Masala hot, garnished with fresh chopped cilantro if desired. Enjoy with steamed rice, naan bread, or your favorite side dishes.

Store any leftovers in an airtight container in the refrigerator for up to 3 days.

Enjoy your homemade Chicken Tikka Masala, a delicious and comforting Indian-inspired dish! Adjust the level of spiciness to suit your taste preferences.

Pork Pie

Ingredients:

For the pastry:

- 2 1/4 cups (280g) all-purpose flour
- 1 teaspoon salt
- 1/2 cup (115g) cold unsalted butter, diced
- 1/4 cup (60g) lard or vegetable shortening, chilled and diced
- 4-6 tablespoons ice water

For the filling:

- 1 lb (450g) ground pork
- 1 small onion, finely chopped
- 1 clove garlic, minced
- 1 teaspoon dried sage
- 1/2 teaspoon dried thyme
- 1/4 teaspoon ground nutmeg
- Salt and pepper, to taste
- 1/4 cup (60ml) chicken or vegetable broth
- 1 tablespoon Worcestershire sauce
- 1 tablespoon all-purpose flour
- 1 egg, beaten (for egg wash)

Instructions:

To make the pastry, sift the flour and salt into a large mixing bowl. Add the diced butter and lard or vegetable shortening. Use a pastry cutter or your fingertips to rub the fats into the flour until the mixture resembles breadcrumbs.
Gradually add the ice water, a tablespoon at a time, mixing with a fork until the dough comes together into a rough ball. You may not need to use all the water.
Turn the dough out onto a lightly floured surface and knead it briefly until smooth. Shape the dough into a disc, wrap it in plastic wrap, and refrigerate for at least 30 minutes.
Meanwhile, prepare the filling. In a skillet, cook the ground pork over medium heat until browned, breaking it up with a spoon as it cooks. Add the chopped onion and minced garlic and cook for another 2-3 minutes until the onion is softened.
Stir in the dried sage, dried thyme, ground nutmeg, salt, and pepper. Cook for another minute until fragrant.
In a small bowl, mix together the chicken or vegetable broth, Worcestershire sauce, and flour until smooth. Pour this mixture into the skillet with the pork, stirring to combine. Cook for another 2-3 minutes until the mixture thickens slightly. Remove from heat and let it cool.
Preheat your oven to 375°F (190°C). Grease a 9-inch (23cm) pie dish or use individual pie tins.

On a lightly floured surface, roll out two-thirds of the pastry dough into a circle large enough to line the pie dish. Gently transfer the pastry to the dish, pressing it into the bottom and up the sides.

Spoon the cooled pork filling into the pastry-lined dish, spreading it out evenly. Roll out the remaining pastry dough into a circle large enough to cover the pie. Place the pastry over the filling and trim any excess. Use a fork to crimp the edges to seal the pie.

Cut a few slits in the top of the pie to allow steam to escape during baking. Brush the pastry with beaten egg for a golden finish.

Bake the pork pie in the preheated oven for 45-50 minutes, or until the pastry is golden brown and crisp.

Once baked, remove the pie from the oven and let it cool in the dish for a few minutes before serving.

Serve the pork pie warm or at room temperature, sliced into wedges. It's delicious on its own or with a side of chutney or mustard.

Enjoy your homemade pork pie, a classic British favorite!

Bubble and Squeak

Ingredients:

- Leftover mashed potatoes
- Leftover cooked cabbage (or other greens such as Brussels sprouts or kale)
- Butter or oil, for frying
- Salt and pepper, to taste

Instructions:

If you don't have leftover mashed potatoes, you can boil potatoes until tender, then mash them with a little butter or milk until smooth.

Similarly, if you don't have leftover cooked cabbage, you can boil or steam cabbage until tender, then chop it finely.

In a large mixing bowl, combine the mashed potatoes and chopped cooked cabbage. Season with salt and pepper to taste.

Heat a little butter or oil in a large frying pan over medium heat.

Once the butter is melted or the oil is hot, add the potato and cabbage mixture to the pan, spreading it out evenly.

Allow the mixture to cook undisturbed for a few minutes until the bottom starts to crisp and turn golden brown.

Use a spatula to carefully flip the bubble and squeak mixture over in sections, ensuring that the crispy bottom side is now facing up.

Continue to cook the bubble and squeak, pressing it down gently with the spatula, until the other side is golden brown and crispy as well.

Once both sides are crispy and golden brown, transfer the bubble and squeak to a serving plate.

Slice the bubble and squeak into wedges or squares, and serve hot as a side dish or light meal.

Bubble and Squeak pairs well with fried eggs, grilled sausages, or bacon for a hearty breakfast or brunch.

Enjoy your homemade Bubble and Squeak, a delicious way to use up leftover vegetables and create a tasty and satisfying dish!

Pork Scratchings

Ingredients:

- Pork skin (from a butcher or pork belly with skin attached)
- Salt, to taste

Instructions:

Preheat your oven to 325°F (160°C).

Start by preparing the pork skin. If you're using pork belly, make sure it still has the skin attached. Alternatively, you can ask your butcher for pork skin specifically for making scratchings.

Using a sharp knife, score the pork skin into small squares or strips. This will help the fat render out and the skin to become crispy during cooking.

Pat the pork skin dry with paper towels to remove any excess moisture. Moisture can prevent the skin from crisping up properly.

Season the pork skin generously with salt. You can also add other seasonings such as paprika, garlic powder, or chili powder for extra flavor if desired.

Place the seasoned pork skin on a baking sheet lined with parchment paper or a wire rack set over a baking sheet. Make sure the pieces of pork skin are spread out in a single layer and not touching each other.

Bake the pork skin in the preheated oven for 1-1.5 hours, or until it is golden brown and crispy. Keep an eye on the pork skin while it's baking to prevent it from burning.

Once the pork skin is crispy and cooked through, remove it from the oven and let it cool slightly.

Serve the pork scratchings warm or at room temperature as a delicious and crunchy snack. They're perfect for enjoying with a cold beer or as part of a charcuterie board.

Store any leftover pork scratchings in an airtight container at room temperature for up to a few days. Enjoy!

Making pork scratchings at home allows you to customize the seasoning and ensures that you're getting a fresh and delicious snack. Experiment with different seasonings to create your perfect batch of pork scratchings.

Mushy Peas

Ingredients:

- 1 cup (200g) dried marrowfat peas

- Water
- Salt, to taste
- Butter (optional)
- Vinegar (optional)

Instructions:

Rinse the dried marrowfat peas under cold water in a sieve or colander to remove any dirt or debris.

Place the peas in a large bowl and cover them with plenty of cold water. Let them soak overnight, or for at least 8 hours. This will soften the peas and reduce their cooking time.

Drain the soaked peas and transfer them to a large saucepan or pot. Add enough fresh water to cover the peas by about 2 inches.

Bring the water to a boil over high heat. Once boiling, reduce the heat to medium-low and let the peas simmer gently for about 30-40 minutes, or until they are very soft and tender.

Once the peas are cooked, drain them well and return them to the saucepan. Use a potato masher or immersion blender to mash or puree the peas until they reach your desired consistency. Some people prefer a smoother texture, while others like to leave some whole peas for texture.

Season the mushy peas with salt to taste. You can also stir in a knob of butter for added richness, if desired.

If you like, you can add a splash of vinegar to the mushy peas for extra flavor. Malt vinegar is a traditional choice, but you can use any type of vinegar you prefer.

Serve the mushy peas hot as a side dish to accompany traditional British meals such as fish and chips, bangers and mash, or pie and mash.

Enjoy your homemade mushy peas, a classic British comfort food dish!

Feel free to adjust the seasoning and texture of the mushy peas according to your preferences. You can also add additional flavorings such as mint or parsley for variation.

Sausage Rolls

Ingredients:

- 1 lb (450g) pork sausage meat
- 1/2 cup (50g) breadcrumbs
- 1 small onion, finely chopped
- 1 clove garlic, minced
- 1 teaspoon dried sage
- 1 teaspoon dried thyme
- Salt and pepper, to taste
- 2 sheets of puff pastry, thawed if frozen
- 1 egg, beaten (for egg wash)
- Sesame seeds or poppy seeds (optional, for garnish)

Instructions:

Preheat your oven to 400°F (200°C) and line a baking sheet with parchment paper.

In a mixing bowl, combine the pork sausage meat, breadcrumbs, chopped onion, minced garlic, dried sage, dried thyme, salt, and pepper. Use your hands to mix everything together until well combined.

On a lightly floured surface, roll out one sheet of puff pastry into a rectangle about 12 inches (30cm) long and 6 inches (15cm) wide.

Cut the rolled-out pastry sheet in half lengthwise to create two long strips.

Divide the sausage mixture in half and shape each half into a long log shape.

Place one sausage log along the center of each pastry strip.

Brush one long edge of each pastry strip with beaten egg.

Roll up the pastry strips tightly around the sausage logs, sealing them shut with the egg-brushed edge.

Repeat the process with the remaining sheet of puff pastry and sausage mixture.

Once both sausage rolls are assembled, use a sharp knife to cut each roll into smaller pieces, about 2 inches (5cm) long.

Place the cut sausage rolls on the prepared baking sheet, leaving some space between each roll.

Brush the tops of the sausage rolls with beaten egg, then sprinkle with sesame seeds or poppy seeds, if desired, for garnish.

Bake the sausage rolls in the preheated oven for 20-25 minutes, or until the pastry is golden brown and cooked through.

Once baked, remove the sausage rolls from the oven and let them cool slightly before serving.
Serve the sausage rolls warm as a delicious snack or appetizer.

Enjoy your homemade sausage rolls, perfect for parties, picnics, or a tasty snack any time of day! You can also customize the recipe by adding herbs, spices, or other flavorings to the sausage meat mixture.

Liver and Onions

Ingredients:

- 4 slices of beef liver (about 1 lb/450g)
- 2 large onions, thinly sliced
- 1/2 cup (60g) all-purpose flour
- Salt and pepper, to taste
- 2 tablespoons vegetable oil or butter
- 1 tablespoon Worcestershire sauce (optional)
- Chopped fresh parsley, for garnish (optional)

Instructions:

Rinse the liver slices under cold water and pat them dry with paper towels.
Season both sides of the liver slices with salt and pepper.
Place the flour in a shallow dish or on a plate. Dredge each liver slice in the flour until evenly coated, shaking off any excess.
Heat the vegetable oil or butter in a large skillet or frying pan over medium heat.
Once the oil is hot, add the sliced onions to the skillet. Cook the onions, stirring occasionally, until they are softened and golden brown, about 10-15 minutes.
Remove the onions from the skillet and set them aside.
In the same skillet, add more oil if needed, and increase the heat to medium-high. Add the flour-coated liver slices to the skillet, being careful not to overcrowd the pan.
Cook the liver slices for 2-3 minutes on each side, or until they are browned on the outside but still slightly pink in the center. Be careful not to overcook the liver, as it can become tough and dry.
If using Worcestershire sauce, you can add it to the skillet along with the liver slices, allowing it to infuse the dish with extra flavor.
Once the liver slices are cooked to your liking, return the cooked onions to the skillet, stirring to combine with the liver.
Reduce the heat to low and let the liver and onions simmer together for a few minutes, allowing the flavors to meld.

Taste the liver and onions and adjust the seasoning with salt and pepper if needed.
Once ready, transfer the liver and onions to a serving platter or individual plates.
Garnish the liver and onions with chopped fresh parsley, if desired, for added color and freshness.
Serve the liver and onions hot, accompanied by mashed potatoes, rice, or crusty bread, and your favorite vegetables.
Enjoy this comforting and hearty dish, rich in flavor and nutrients!

Liver and onions is a nutritious dish packed with protein, iron, and other essential nutrients. It's a classic comfort food that can be enjoyed for lunch or dinner. Adjust the seasoning and cooking time according to your preferences for a dish that's just right for you.

Black Pudding

Ingredients:

- 1 pint (about 475ml) fresh pig's blood (you may need to ask your butcher for this)
- 1 cup (120g) steel-cut oats or medium oatmeal
- 1 onion, finely chopped
- 1/2 cup (120ml) pork fat (lard), diced
- 1 teaspoon salt
- 1/2 teaspoon ground black pepper
- 1/2 teaspoon ground cloves
- 1/2 teaspoon ground nutmeg
- 1/2 teaspoon ground allspice

Instructions:

In a large mixing bowl, combine the fresh pig's blood, steel-cut oats, finely chopped onion, diced pork fat, salt, black pepper, ground cloves, ground nutmeg, and ground allspice. Mix well to combine all the ingredients thoroughly.

If the mixture seems too dry, you can add a little water to achieve a looser consistency, but be careful not to add too much.

Once the mixture is well combined, pour it into a large sausage casing or synthetic casing. Tie off the ends securely with kitchen twine.

Bring a large pot of water to a gentle simmer. Carefully add the black pudding sausage to the pot, ensuring that it is fully submerged in the water.

Let the black pudding sausage simmer gently for 1-2 hours, maintaining a low heat and turning the sausage occasionally to ensure even cooking.

After 1-2 hours, remove the black pudding sausage from the pot and let it cool slightly.

Once cooled, carefully remove the casing from the black pudding sausage. You can slice the black pudding into rounds or wedges, as desired.

Heat a skillet or frying pan over medium heat. Add a little butter or oil to the pan, then fry the black pudding slices for a few minutes on each side until they are crispy and heated through.
Once cooked, remove the black pudding slices from the pan and serve hot, accompanied by traditional British breakfast items such as fried eggs, bacon, grilled tomatoes, and toast.
Enjoy your homemade black pudding, a classic British delicacy rich in flavor and history!

Black pudding can also be enjoyed in a variety of other ways, such as in stews, pies, or even as part of a charcuterie board. Adjust the seasonings and spices according to your taste preferences, and feel free to experiment with different fillers such as barley or breadcrumbs.

Scotch Broth

Ingredients:

- 1 lb (450g) lamb or beef stew meat, diced
- 1 cup (200g) pearl barley, rinsed
- 1 onion, chopped
- 2 carrots, diced
- 2 celery stalks, diced
- 2 cloves garlic, minced
- 8 cups (1.9 liters) beef or lamb broth
- 2 bay leaves
- 1 teaspoon dried thyme
- 1 teaspoon dried rosemary
- Salt and pepper, to taste
- Chopped fresh parsley, for garnish (optional)

Instructions:

In a large soup pot or Dutch oven, heat a little oil over medium-high heat. Add the diced lamb or beef and brown it on all sides, stirring occasionally.
Once the meat is browned, add the chopped onion, diced carrots, diced celery, and minced garlic to the pot. Cook for a few minutes until the vegetables start to soften.

Add the rinsed pearl barley to the pot, followed by the beef or lamb broth. Stir well to combine.

Add the bay leaves, dried thyme, and dried rosemary to the pot, stirring to distribute the herbs evenly.

Season the broth with salt and pepper, to taste.

Bring the broth to a boil, then reduce the heat to low and let the soup simmer gently, partially covered, for about 1 to 1.5 hours, or until the meat is tender and the barley is cooked through. Stir occasionally and skim off any foam or excess fat that rises to the surface.

Once the soup is ready, taste and adjust the seasoning if needed.

Ladle the Scotch broth into serving bowls and garnish with chopped fresh parsley, if desired.

Serve the Scotch broth hot, accompanied by crusty bread or rolls for a comforting and nourishing meal.

Enjoy your homemade Scotch broth, a hearty and delicious soup perfect for cold days!

Feel free to customize the Scotch broth according to your preferences. You can add other vegetables such as potatoes, turnips, or leeks, and adjust the herbs and seasonings to suit your taste. This soup is also a great way to use up leftover meat and vegetables.

Pea and Ham Soup

Ingredients:

- 1 cup (200g) dried split peas, rinsed and drained
- 1 ham hock or ham bone
- 1 onion, chopped
- 2 carrots, chopped
- 2 celery stalks, chopped
- 2 cloves garlic, minced
- 6 cups (1.4 liters) chicken or vegetable broth
- 1 bay leaf
- 1 teaspoon dried thyme
- Salt and pepper, to taste
- Chopped fresh parsley, for garnish (optional)

Instructions:

In a large soup pot or Dutch oven, combine the dried split peas, ham hock or ham bone, chopped onion, chopped carrots, chopped celery, minced garlic, chicken or vegetable broth, bay leaf, and dried thyme.

Bring the mixture to a boil over medium-high heat, then reduce the heat to low. Cover the pot and let the soup simmer gently for about 1.5 to 2 hours, or until the split peas are tender and the meat on the ham hock or bone is falling off the bone.

Once the soup is cooked, remove the ham hock or bone from the pot and set it aside to cool slightly.

Use an immersion blender or transfer a portion of the soup to a blender to puree until smooth. Be careful when blending hot liquids.

Shred the meat from the ham hock or bone, discarding any excess fat or skin. Return the shredded ham to the pot.

Season the soup with salt and pepper, to taste, adjusting the seasoning as needed.

If the soup is too thick, you can thin it out with a little more broth or water until you reach your desired consistency.

Ladle the pea and ham soup into serving bowls and garnish with chopped fresh parsley, if desired.

Serve the soup hot, accompanied by crusty bread or rolls for a delicious and satisfying meal.

Enjoy your homemade pea and ham soup, a comforting dish that's perfect for warming you up on chilly days!

Feel free to customize the soup according to your preferences. You can add other vegetables such as potatoes or leeks, or experiment with different herbs and seasonings to suit your taste. This soup also freezes well, so you can make a big batch and save some for later.

Steak and Kidney Pie

Ingredients:

For the filling:

- 1 lb (450g) beef steak, cut into bite-sized pieces
- 1/2 lb (225g) beef kidneys, cleaned and diced
- 1 onion, chopped
- 2 carrots, diced
- 2 celery stalks, diced
- 2 cloves garlic, minced
- 2 tablespoons all-purpose flour
- 2 cups (480ml) beef broth
- 1 tablespoon Worcestershire sauce

- 1 teaspoon dried thyme
- Salt and pepper, to taste
- 2 tablespoons vegetable oil or butter

For the pastry crust:

- 2 cups (250g) all-purpose flour
- 1/2 teaspoon salt
- 1/2 cup (115g) cold butter, diced
- 4-6 tablespoons cold water

Instructions:

Preheat your oven to 375°F (190°C).
In a large skillet or frying pan, heat the vegetable oil or butter over medium-high heat. Add the diced beef steak and beef kidneys to the skillet and cook until browned on all sides. Remove the browned meat from the skillet and set it aside.
In the same skillet, add the chopped onion, diced carrots, and diced celery. Cook until the vegetables are softened, about 5 minutes. Add the minced garlic and cook for an additional minute until fragrant.
Sprinkle the flour over the vegetables in the skillet and stir to coat evenly. Cook for another minute to cook off the raw flour taste.
Gradually pour in the beef broth, stirring constantly to prevent lumps from forming. Add the Worcestershire sauce, dried thyme, salt, and pepper. Stir well to combine.
Return the browned beef steak and kidneys to the skillet. Bring the mixture to a simmer, then cover the skillet and let it simmer gently for about 1 to 1.5 hours, or until the meat is tender and the sauce has thickened.
While the filling is simmering, prepare the pastry crust. In a large mixing bowl, combine the all-purpose flour and salt. Add the diced cold butter to the flour mixture and use a pastry cutter or your fingers to rub the butter into the flour until the mixture resembles coarse crumbs.
Gradually add the cold water to the flour mixture, stirring with a fork until a dough forms. Be careful not to overmix.

Divide the pastry dough into two portions, one slightly larger than the other. Roll out the larger portion of pastry dough on a lightly floured surface to fit the base and sides of a pie dish.

Transfer the rolled-out pastry dough to the pie dish, pressing it gently into the base and sides. Trim any excess dough from the edges.

Once the filling is ready, pour it into the prepared pie dish over the pastry crust.

Roll out the remaining portion of pastry dough to fit the top of the pie. Place it over the filling, pressing the edges to seal with the bottom crust. Trim any excess dough from the edges.

Use a sharp knife to make a few slits in the top crust to allow steam to escape during baking.

Optional: Brush the top crust with beaten egg for a shiny finish.

Place the pie dish on a baking sheet to catch any drips, then transfer it to the preheated oven.

Bake the steak and kidney pie in the oven for 30-40 minutes, or until the pastry is golden brown and cooked through.

Once baked, remove the pie from the oven and let it cool for a few minutes before serving.

Serve the steak and kidney pie hot, accompanied by mashed potatoes, peas, or your favorite side dishes.

Enjoy your homemade steak and kidney pie, a comforting and flavorful British classic!

Adjust the seasoning and ingredients according to your taste preferences.

Spotted Dick

Ingredients:

- 1 cup (150g) self-raising flour
- 1/2 cup (100g) shredded suet (vegetarian suet can be used for a meat-free version)
- 1/2 cup (100g) caster sugar
- 1/2 cup (75g) dried currants or raisins
- Zest of 1 lemon

- Pinch of salt
- Milk, to bind (approximately 4-6 tablespoons)
- Custard, to serve

Instructions:

In a mixing bowl, combine the self-raising flour, shredded suet, caster sugar, dried currants or raisins, lemon zest, and a pinch of salt. Mix well to combine all the ingredients evenly.
Gradually add the milk to the dry ingredients, a little at a time, stirring with a spoon until a soft dough forms. You may not need to use all the milk, so add it gradually until the dough comes together.
Once the dough has formed, turn it out onto a lightly floured surface and knead it gently for a minute or two until smooth.
Shape the dough into a log shape, about 8 inches (20cm) long and 2 inches (5cm) in diameter.
Tear off a large sheet of parchment paper and place the dough log in the center. Roll up the parchment paper tightly around the dough, twisting the ends to seal.
Bring a large pot of water to a gentle simmer. Carefully lower the wrapped Spotted Dick into the pot, ensuring that it is fully submerged in the water.
Let the Spotted Dick simmer gently for about 1.5 to 2 hours, turning it occasionally, or until it is firm and cooked through. Check the water level occasionally and top up with more boiling water if needed.
Once cooked, carefully remove the Spotted Dick from the pot and let it cool slightly. Unwrap the parchment paper and transfer the Spotted Dick to a serving plate.
Slice the Spotted Dick into thick rounds and serve warm with custard poured over the top.
Enjoy your homemade Spotted Dick, a classic British dessert that's rich, comforting, and perfect for any occasion!

Feel free to customize the Spotted Dick by adding spices such as cinnamon or nutmeg to the dough, or substituting the dried currants or raisins with other dried fruits such as sultanas or chopped apricots.

Sticky Toffee Pudding

Ingredients:

For the pudding:

- 1 cup (200g) chopped dates
- 1 cup (240ml) boiling water
- 1 teaspoon baking soda
- 1 and 1/2 cups (190g) all-purpose flour
- 1 teaspoon baking powder
- 1/2 teaspoon salt
- 1/2 cup (115g) unsalted butter, softened
- 3/4 cup (150g) granulated sugar
- 2 large eggs
- 1 teaspoon vanilla extract

For the toffee sauce:

- 1 cup (200g) dark brown sugar
- 1/2 cup (115g) unsalted butter
- 1 cup (240ml) heavy cream
- 1 teaspoon vanilla extract
- Pinch of salt

Instructions:

Preheat your oven to 350°F (175°C). Grease a 9x9 inch (23x23cm) square baking dish or individual ramekins.
In a bowl, combine the chopped dates and boiling water. Stir in the baking soda and let it sit for about 10 minutes.
In a separate bowl, whisk together the flour, baking powder, and salt.
In a large mixing bowl, cream together the softened butter and granulated sugar until light and fluffy.
Beat in the eggs, one at a time, followed by the vanilla extract.
Gradually add the dry ingredients to the wet ingredients, mixing until just combined.
Fold in the soaked dates along with any remaining liquid.
Pour the batter into the prepared baking dish or divide evenly among the ramekins.
Bake in the preheated oven for 25-30 minutes (or 15-20 minutes for individual portions), or until a toothpick inserted into the center comes out clean.

While the pudding is baking, prepare the toffee sauce. In a saucepan, combine the dark brown sugar, unsalted butter, heavy cream, vanilla extract, and salt. Cook over medium heat, stirring constantly, until the mixture comes to a simmer and thickens slightly, about 5-7 minutes.

Remove the saucepan from the heat and let the toffee sauce cool slightly.

Once the pudding is baked, remove it from the oven and poke holes all over the top using a skewer or fork.

Pour half of the warm toffee sauce over the top of the pudding, allowing it to seep into the holes.

Serve the sticky toffee pudding warm, drizzled with extra toffee sauce and topped with whipped cream or vanilla ice cream, if desired.

Enjoy your homemade sticky toffee pudding, a decadent and indulgent dessert that's perfect for any occasion!

Eton Mess

Ingredients:

- 4 large egg whites, at room temperature
- 1 cup (200g) granulated sugar
- 1 teaspoon white vinegar or lemon juice
- 1 teaspoon cornstarch (cornflour)
- 1 cup (240ml) heavy cream
- 2 tablespoons powdered sugar (icing sugar)
- 1 teaspoon vanilla extract
- 2 cups (about 300g) fresh strawberries, hulled and sliced
- Additional strawberries for garnish (optional)
- Mint leaves for garnish (optional)

Instructions:

Preheat your oven to 250°F (120°C). Line a baking sheet with parchment paper.
In a clean, dry mixing bowl, beat the egg whites with an electric mixer on medium speed until soft peaks form.
Gradually add the granulated sugar, 1 tablespoon at a time, while continuing to beat the egg whites. Once all the sugar has been added, increase the speed to high and beat until stiff, glossy peaks form.
Add the white vinegar or lemon juice and cornstarch to the meringue mixture, and gently fold them in with a spatula until well combined.
Spoon dollops of the meringue onto the prepared baking sheet, forming small nests or pavlovas. You should have enough meringue for about 8 small nests.
Bake the meringues in the preheated oven for 1 hour, or until they are dry and crisp on the outside. Turn off the oven and let the meringues cool completely inside with the oven door closed.
While the meringues are cooling, prepare the whipped cream. In a mixing bowl, beat the heavy cream, powdered sugar, and vanilla extract together until stiff peaks form.
Crush half of the cooled meringues into small pieces, leaving the other half whole or in larger chunks for texture.
In serving glasses or bowls, layer the crushed meringue, whipped cream, and sliced strawberries, repeating the layers until the glasses are filled.

Garnish the Eton Mess with additional sliced strawberries and mint leaves, if desired.
Serve the Eton Mess immediately, as the meringue will soften if left to sit for too long.
Enjoy your homemade Eton Mess, a delightful dessert that's perfect for summer gatherings and celebrations!

Trifle

Ingredients:

- 1 sponge cake or pound cake, sliced (or enough ladyfingers to cover the bottom of your trifle dish)
- 1/2 cup (120ml) sherry or fruit juice (optional, for soaking the cake)
- 2 cups (480ml) custard (you can use homemade or store-bought)
- 2 cups (480ml) whipped cream
- 2 cups (about 300g) mixed fresh fruit (such as berries, kiwi, or bananas), sliced or chopped
- 1/4 cup (50g) granulated sugar (optional, for sweetening the fruit)
- 1/4 cup (25g) sliced almonds or grated chocolate, for garnish (optional)
- Fresh mint leaves, for garnish (optional)

Instructions:

If using sponge cake or pound cake, slice it into thin slices. Arrange the cake slices in the bottom of a trifle dish, covering the entire bottom. If desired, drizzle the sherry or fruit juice over the cake slices to moisten them.
Prepare the custard according to the recipe or package instructions. Allow it to cool slightly before assembling the trifle.
Once the custard has cooled, pour it over the cake layer in the trifle dish, spreading it out evenly with a spatula.
Next, layer the mixed fresh fruit on top of the custard layer. If using bananas, toss them in a little lemon juice to prevent browning.
If desired, sprinkle granulated sugar over the fruit to sweeten it slightly.
Spread the whipped cream over the fruit layer, covering it completely.
Garnish the top of the trifle with sliced almonds or grated chocolate, if desired.
Refrigerate the trifle for at least 2 hours, or until chilled and set.
Before serving, garnish the trifle with fresh mint leaves for a pop of color and freshness.
Serve the trifle cold, scooping out portions into individual bowls.

Enjoy your homemade trifle, a delicious and elegant dessert perfect for any occasion!

Feel free to customize the trifle with your favorite ingredients. You can use different flavors of cake, swap the custard for pudding, or add layers of jam or jelly for extra flavor. Get creative and have fun experimenting with different combinations!

Apple Crumble

Ingredients:

For the filling:

- 4-5 medium-sized apples (such as Granny Smith), peeled, cored, and sliced
- 1/4 cup (50g) granulated sugar
- 1 tablespoon lemon juice
- 1 teaspoon ground cinnamon
- 1/4 teaspoon ground nutmeg (optional)
- 1 tablespoon all-purpose flour (optional, to thicken the filling)

For the crumble topping:

- 1 cup (120g) all-purpose flour
- 1/2 cup (100g) granulated sugar
- 1/2 cup (115g) unsalted butter, cold, cut into small cubes
- 1/2 cup (40g) rolled oats (optional, for added texture)
- Pinch of salt

Instructions:

Preheat your oven to 375°F (190°C). Grease a 9-inch (23cm) square baking dish or similar-sized pie dish.
In a large mixing bowl, toss the sliced apples with the granulated sugar, lemon juice, ground cinnamon, ground nutmeg (if using), and all-purpose flour (if using). Make sure the apples are evenly coated with the sugar and spices.

Transfer the coated apples to the prepared baking dish, spreading them out into an even layer.

In the same mixing bowl (no need to clean it), combine the all-purpose flour, granulated sugar, and pinch of salt for the crumble topping. Add the cold cubed butter.

Using your fingertips or a pastry cutter, work the butter into the dry ingredients until the mixture resembles coarse crumbs. Some larger pea-sized pieces of butter are fine; they will help create a flaky and crispy texture.

If using rolled oats, mix them into the crumble topping mixture.

Sprinkle the crumble topping evenly over the apples in the baking dish, covering them completely.

Place the baking dish in the preheated oven and bake for 35-40 minutes, or until the topping is golden brown and the apples are tender and bubbling.

Remove the apple crumble from the oven and let it cool slightly before serving.

Serve the apple crumble warm, optionally with a scoop of vanilla ice cream or a dollop of whipped cream on top.

Enjoy your homemade apple crumble, a comforting and delicious dessert perfect for any occasion!

Feel free to customize your apple crumble by adding nuts (such as chopped pecans or walnuts) to the topping, or by mixing in other fruits (such as berries or rhubarb) with the apples for a variation on the classic recipe.

Bread and Butter Pudding

Ingredients:

- 6-8 slices of bread (preferably slightly stale)
- Butter, softened
- 3 eggs
- 2 cups (500ml) milk
- 1/2 cup (100g) sugar
- 1 teaspoon vanilla extract
- 1/2 teaspoon ground cinnamon (optional)
- 1/4 cup raisins or sultanas (optional)
- Nutmeg, for sprinkling

Instructions:

Preheat your oven to 350°F (175°C). Grease a baking dish with butter or non-stick spray.
Butter the bread slices on one side and cut them into triangles or squares.
Arrange a layer of bread slices, buttered side up, in the bottom of the prepared baking dish. Sprinkle with raisins or sultanas if using.
In a mixing bowl, whisk together the eggs, milk, sugar, vanilla extract, and cinnamon until well combined.
Pour half of the custard mixture over the bread slices, ensuring they are evenly soaked.

Add another layer of buttered bread slices on top, then pour the remaining custard mixture over them.
Allow the pudding to sit for about 10-15 minutes to let the bread absorb the custard.
Sprinkle the top with nutmeg for flavor.
Place the baking dish in a larger roasting pan and pour hot water into the roasting pan until it comes about halfway up the sides of the baking dish. This water bath helps the pudding cook evenly and prevents it from curdling.
Bake in the preheated oven for 45-50 minutes, or until the custard is set and the top is golden brown and crispy.
Once done, remove from the oven and let it cool for a few minutes before serving.
Serve warm, either plain or with a dollop of whipped cream, custard, or vanilla ice cream, if desired.

Enjoy your delicious homemade bread and butter pudding!

Roast Beef with Yorkshire Pudding

Ingredients:

For the roast beef:

- 3-4 pounds (1.5-2 kg) beef roast (such as ribeye, sirloin, or tenderloin)
- Salt and freshly ground black pepper
- Olive oil or beef drippings

For the Yorkshire pudding:

- 1 cup (125g) all-purpose flour
- 1 cup (240ml) whole milk
- 3 large eggs
- Pinch of salt
- Beef drippings or vegetable oil

Instructions:

For the roast beef:

Preheat your oven to 425°F (220°C).

Pat the beef roast dry with paper towels and season it generously with salt and freshly ground black pepper.

Heat a roasting pan over medium-high heat on the stovetop. Add a little olive oil or beef drippings to the pan.

Once the pan is hot, sear the beef roast on all sides until nicely browned, about 2-3 minutes per side.

Transfer the roasting pan to the preheated oven and roast the beef for about 15 minutes per pound (450g) for medium-rare, or until it reaches your desired level of doneness. Use a meat thermometer to check for an internal temperature of 130-135°F (55-57°C) for medium-rare, or adjust according to your preference.

Once done, remove the roast from the oven and let it rest for at least 15 minutes before slicing.

For the Yorkshire pudding:

While the beef is roasting, prepare the Yorkshire pudding batter. In a mixing bowl, whisk together the flour, milk, eggs, and a pinch of salt until smooth. Let the batter rest at room temperature for at least 30 minutes.

After removing the roast from the oven, increase the oven temperature to 450°F (230°C).

Pour the beef drippings or a little vegetable oil into a muffin tin or a large baking dish. Place the tin or dish in the oven to heat up for about 5 minutes.

Carefully remove the hot tin or dish from the oven, and quickly pour the Yorkshire pudding batter into the hot drippings or oil, filling each cup or covering the bottom of the dish.

Place the tin or dish back in the oven and bake the Yorkshire puddings for about 20-25 minutes, or until puffed up and golden brown.

Serve the roast beef sliced thinly alongside the Yorkshire puddings, along with your favorite gravy and accompaniments such as roasted vegetables or mashed potatoes.

Enjoy your delicious roast beef with Yorkshire pudding!

Chicken and Leek Pie

Ingredients:

For the filling:

- 2 tablespoons butter
- 1 onion, finely chopped
- 2 leeks, washed and sliced
- 2 cloves garlic, minced
- 2 tablespoons all-purpose flour
- 1 1/2 cups (360ml) chicken stock
- 1/2 cup (120ml) heavy cream
- 2 cups cooked chicken, shredded or diced
- Salt and pepper, to taste
- 1/4 cup fresh parsley, chopped
- Optional: 1 cup frozen peas or mixed vegetables

For the pastry:

- 1 sheet of puff pastry, thawed if frozen
- 1 egg, beaten (for egg wash)

Instructions:

Preheat your oven to 375°F (190°C).
In a large skillet or saucepan, melt the butter over medium heat. Add the chopped onion and sliced leeks, and cook until softened, about 5-7 minutes.
Add the minced garlic to the pan and cook for another minute until fragrant.
Sprinkle the flour over the vegetables and stir well to combine. Cook for a minute or two to cook out the raw flour taste.
Gradually pour in the chicken stock, stirring constantly to prevent lumps from forming. Once the mixture has thickened slightly, stir in the heavy cream.
Add the cooked chicken to the sauce, along with salt, pepper, and chopped parsley. If using frozen peas or mixed vegetables, add them now. Stir well to combine and let the filling simmer gently for a few minutes until everything is heated through. Taste and adjust seasoning if needed.
Transfer the chicken and leek filling into a pie dish or individual ramekins.
Roll out the puff pastry on a lightly floured surface to fit the size of your pie dish or ramekins. Place the pastry over the filling, pressing down the edges to seal.
Use a sharp knife to make a few small slits in the pastry to allow steam to escape during baking.
Brush the pastry with beaten egg to give it a golden finish.
Place the pie dish or ramekins on a baking sheet (to catch any drips) and bake in the preheated oven for 25-30 minutes, or until the pastry is puffed and golden brown.
Remove from the oven and let the pie cool for a few minutes before serving.

Serve your delicious chicken and leek pie hot, with your favorite sides such as mashed potatoes and steamed vegetables. Enjoy!

Chicken Curry

Ingredients:

- 1.5 lbs (about 700g) boneless, skinless chicken thighs or breasts, cut into bite-sized pieces
- 2 tablespoons vegetable oil or ghee
- 1 large onion, finely chopped
- 3 cloves garlic, minced
- 1-inch piece of ginger, grated
- 2 tomatoes, chopped
- 1-2 green chilies, slit (optional, adjust to taste)
- 1 teaspoon ground turmeric
- 2 teaspoons ground coriander
- 1 teaspoon ground cumin
- 1 teaspoon paprika or chili powder (adjust to taste)
- 1 teaspoon garam masala
- Salt to taste

- 1 cup (240ml) coconut milk or yogurt
- Fresh cilantro (coriander leaves) for garnish
- Cooked rice or naan bread, for serving

Instructions:

Heat the oil or ghee in a large skillet or pot over medium heat. Add the chopped onions and cook until they turn soft and translucent, about 5-7 minutes.

Add the minced garlic and grated ginger to the skillet, and cook for another 1-2 minutes until fragrant.

Stir in the chopped tomatoes and green chilies (if using), and cook until the tomatoes break down and become mushy.

Add the ground turmeric, coriander, cumin, paprika or chili powder, garam masala, and salt to the skillet. Stir well to combine and cook for a minute to toast the spices.

Add the chicken pieces to the skillet and coat them evenly with the spice mixture. Cook for 5-7 minutes, stirring occasionally, until the chicken is lightly browned on all sides.

Pour in the coconut milk or yogurt, stirring well to combine. Reduce the heat to low, cover the skillet, and let the curry simmer gently for 15-20 minutes, or until the chicken is cooked through and the flavors have melded together.

Taste the curry and adjust seasoning if needed. If the curry is too thick, you can add a little water or chicken broth to reach your desired consistency.

Once the chicken is cooked and the curry has reached your desired consistency, remove the skillet from the heat.

Garnish the chicken curry with fresh cilantro leaves before serving.

Serve the chicken curry hot with cooked rice or naan bread on the side.

Enjoy your delicious homemade chicken curry! Feel free to customize the recipe by adding vegetables like potatoes, carrots, or bell peppers if you like.

Gammon Steak with Pineapple

Ingredients:

- 2 gammon steaks (about 8 oz each)
- 1 tablespoon olive oil or butter
- Salt and pepper, to taste
- 4 pineapple slices (fresh or canned)
- 2 tablespoons brown sugar (optional, for caramelizing the pineapple)
- Fresh parsley or chives, chopped (for garnish, optional)

Instructions:

If using canned pineapple slices, drain them well. If using fresh pineapple, peel and core it, then slice it into rings.

Preheat your grill or grill pan to medium-high heat.

Brush the gammon steaks with olive oil or melted butter on both sides, and season them with salt and pepper.

Place the gammon steaks on the grill or grill pan and cook for about 4-5 minutes on each side, or until they are cooked through and have nice grill marks. The internal temperature should reach 145°F (63°C).

While the gammon steaks are cooking, you can prepare the pineapple slices. If desired, sprinkle brown sugar over each pineapple slice to help caramelize them.

Place the pineapple slices on the grill or grill pan alongside the gammon steaks. Cook for about 2-3 minutes on each side, or until they are caramelized and have grill marks.

Once the gammon steaks and pineapple slices are cooked, transfer them to a serving plate.

Garnish with chopped parsley or chives, if desired, for a fresh touch.

Serve the gammon steaks with the caramelized pineapple slices alongside. You can also serve it with your choice of side dishes, such as mashed potatoes, steamed vegetables, or a simple salad.

Enjoy your delicious gammon steak with pineapple!

Beef and Ale Stew

Ingredients:

- 2 pounds (about 900g) stewing beef, cut into chunks
- 2 tablespoons all-purpose flour
- Salt and pepper, to taste
- 2 tablespoons vegetable oil or olive oil
- 1 large onion, diced

- 2 cloves garlic, minced
- 2 carrots, peeled and diced
- 2 celery stalks, diced
- 2 tablespoons tomato paste
- 2 cups (480ml) beef broth
- 1 bottle (12 ounces/355ml) of ale or stout beer
- 2 bay leaves
- 1 teaspoon dried thyme (or 2-3 sprigs of fresh thyme)
- 2 cups (about 300g) potatoes, peeled and diced
- Chopped fresh parsley, for garnish (optional)

Instructions:

In a large bowl, toss the beef chunks with the flour, salt, and pepper until evenly coated.

Heat the vegetable oil or olive oil in a large pot or Dutch oven over medium-high heat. Add the beef in batches and brown it on all sides. Don't overcrowd the pot, as this will prevent proper browning. Remove the browned beef and set it aside.

In the same pot, add the diced onion, garlic, carrots, and celery. Cook, stirring occasionally, until the vegetables are softened, about 5-7 minutes.

Stir in the tomato paste and cook for another 2 minutes, stirring constantly.

Return the browned beef to the pot. Pour in the beef broth and ale (or stout beer), scraping the bottom of the pot to loosen any browned bits.

Add the bay leaves and dried thyme (or fresh thyme sprigs) to the pot. Bring the stew to a simmer, then reduce the heat to low. Cover and let it simmer gently for about 1 1/2 to 2 hours, or until the beef is tender and the flavors have melded together.

Add the diced potatoes to the stew and continue to simmer, uncovered, for another 30 minutes, or until the potatoes are cooked through and the stew has thickened slightly. If the stew becomes too thick, you can add more beef broth or water to reach your desired consistency.

Taste the stew and adjust the seasoning with salt and pepper, if needed.

Once the stew is ready, remove the bay leaves and thyme sprigs, if using.

Serve the beef and ale stew hot, garnished with chopped fresh parsley, if desired. It pairs well with crusty bread, mashed potatoes, or a simple green salad.

Enjoy your hearty and delicious beef and ale stew!

Fish Pie

Ingredients:

For the filling:

- 1 lb (450g) mixed fish fillets (such as cod, haddock, salmon), cut into chunks
- 1 onion, finely chopped
- 2 cloves garlic, minced
- 2 tablespoons butter
- 2 tablespoons all-purpose flour
- 1 1/2 cups (360ml) fish or vegetable stock
- 1/2 cup (120ml) heavy cream
- 1 cup (150g) frozen peas
- 2 tablespoons chopped fresh parsley
- Salt and pepper, to taste
- Lemon juice, to taste (optional)

For the mashed potato topping:

- 2 lbs (900g) potatoes, peeled and cut into chunks
- 4 tablespoons butter
- 1/2 cup (120ml) milk or cream
- Salt and pepper, to taste
- Grated cheese (optional, for topping)

Instructions:

Preheat your oven to 375°F (190°C).

Place the potato chunks in a large pot of salted water. Bring to a boil and cook until the potatoes are tender, about 15-20 minutes. Drain the potatoes and return them to the pot.

Mash the potatoes with butter, milk or cream until smooth and creamy. Season with salt and pepper to taste. Set aside.

In a separate saucepan, melt the butter over medium heat. Add the chopped onion and minced garlic, and cook until softened, about 5 minutes.

Stir in the flour and cook for another minute, stirring constantly.

Gradually pour in the fish or vegetable stock, stirring constantly to prevent lumps from forming. Bring to a simmer and cook until the sauce has thickened, about 5 minutes.

Stir in the heavy cream, frozen peas, chopped parsley, and season with salt and pepper to taste. If desired, add a squeeze of lemon juice for extra flavor.

Add the mixed fish fillets to the sauce, stirring gently to combine. Cook for 2-3 minutes, or until the fish is just cooked through. Remove from heat.

Transfer the fish mixture to a baking dish or individual ramekins.

Spread the mashed potatoes over the top of the fish mixture, smoothing it out with a spatula.

If desired, sprinkle grated cheese over the mashed potatoes for extra flavor.

Place the baking dish or ramekins in the preheated oven and bake for 25-30 minutes, or until the top is golden brown and the filling is bubbling.

Remove from the oven and let it cool for a few minutes before serving.

Serve your delicious fish pie hot, with additional chopped parsley sprinkled on top if desired. Enjoy!

Smoked Haddock and Poached Eggs

Ingredients:

- 2 smoked haddock fillets
- 4 large eggs
- 1 tablespoon white vinegar
- Salt and pepper, to taste
- Chopped fresh parsley, for garnish (optional)
- Lemon wedges, for serving (optional)
- Toast or crusty bread, for serving

Instructions:

Prepare the smoked haddock: If the smoked haddock fillets are frozen, thaw them in the refrigerator overnight. Pat them dry with paper towels to remove excess moisture.

Poach the eggs: Fill a large skillet or shallow pan with water and bring it to a gentle simmer over medium heat. Add the white vinegar to the water, which helps the eggs to hold their shape.

Crack each egg into a small cup or ramekin. Using a spoon, create a gentle whirlpool in the simmering water. Carefully slide each egg into the center of the whirlpool. This helps the egg white to wrap around the yolk.

Let the eggs poach for about 3-4 minutes, or until the whites are set but the yolks are still runny. Use a slotted spoon to carefully lift the poached eggs out of the water and transfer them to a plate lined with paper towels to drain excess water.

Cook the smoked haddock: In a separate skillet, add a small amount of butter or olive oil over medium heat. Once hot, add the smoked haddock fillets, skin-side down if applicable. Cook for about 3-4 minutes on each side, or until the fish is cooked through and flakes easily with a fork. Season with salt and pepper to taste.

Assemble the dish: Place the cooked smoked haddock fillets on serving plates. Top each fillet with a poached egg.

Garnish and serve: Sprinkle chopped fresh parsley over the poached eggs for a pop of color and freshness. Serve the smoked haddock and poached eggs with lemon wedges on the side for squeezing over the fish, if desired. Serve with toast or crusty bread on the side.

Enjoy: Serve immediately while the eggs are still warm and runny, and the smoked haddock is tender and flavorful.

This dish makes for a satisfying and elegant breakfast or brunch option. Enjoy!

Beef Bourguignon

Ingredients:

- 2 pounds (about 900g) beef chuck or stewing beef, cut into cubes
- Salt and pepper, to taste
- 2 tablespoons olive oil or vegetable oil
- 4 slices of bacon, chopped
- 1 onion, chopped
- 2 carrots, peeled and sliced
- 2 cloves garlic, minced
- 2 tablespoons all-purpose flour
- 1 bottle (750ml) of red wine, preferably Burgundy or Pinot Noir
- 2 cups (480ml) beef broth
- 2 bay leaves
- 1 teaspoon dried thyme (or 2-3 sprigs of fresh thyme)
- 1 pound (about 450g) mushrooms, sliced
- 1 tablespoon tomato paste
- Chopped fresh parsley, for garnish (optional)

Instructions:

Preheat your oven to 325°F (160°C).

Pat the beef cubes dry with paper towels and season them with salt and pepper.

Heat the olive oil or vegetable oil in a large Dutch oven or oven-safe pot over medium-high heat. Add the beef cubes in batches and brown them on all sides. Remove the browned beef and set it aside.

In the same pot, add the chopped bacon and cook until crispy. Remove the bacon from the pot and set it aside with the beef.

Add the chopped onion and sliced carrots to the pot. Cook, stirring occasionally, until the vegetables are softened, about 5-7 minutes.

Add the minced garlic to the pot and cook for another minute until fragrant.

Sprinkle the flour over the vegetables and stir well to coat. Cook for another minute to cook out the raw flour taste.

Gradually pour in the red wine and beef broth, stirring constantly to prevent lumps from forming. Add the bay leaves and dried thyme to the pot.

Return the browned beef and bacon to the pot. Bring the mixture to a simmer. Cover the pot with a lid and transfer it to the preheated oven. Let it braise in the oven for about 2-2 ½ hours, or until the beef is tender and the flavors have melded together.

In the meantime, heat a separate skillet over medium heat. Add a little oil if needed, then add the sliced mushrooms. Cook the mushrooms until they are browned and tender, about 5-7 minutes. Season with salt and pepper to taste.

Once the beef is tender, remove the pot from the oven. Stir in the cooked mushrooms and tomato paste. Taste and adjust seasoning if needed.

Serve the Beef Bourguignon hot, garnished with chopped fresh parsley if desired. It pairs well with mashed potatoes, crusty bread, or egg noodles.

Enjoy your delicious homemade Beef Bourguignon!

Chicken and Mushroom Pie

Ingredients:

For the filling:

- 2 tablespoons butter
- 1 onion, finely chopped
- 2 cloves garlic, minced
- 8 ounces (225g) mushrooms, sliced
- 2 boneless, skinless chicken breasts, diced
- 2 tablespoons all-purpose flour
- 1 cup (240ml) chicken broth
- 1/2 cup (120ml) heavy cream
- 1 teaspoon dried thyme (or 1 tablespoon fresh thyme leaves)
- Salt and pepper, to taste
- 1/4 cup chopped fresh parsley

For the pastry:

- 1 sheet of puff pastry, thawed if frozen
- 1 egg, beaten (for egg wash)

Instructions:

Preheat your oven to 375°F (190°C).
In a large skillet, melt the butter over medium heat. Add the chopped onion and minced garlic, and cook until softened, about 5 minutes.

Add the sliced mushrooms to the skillet and cook until they release their moisture and become golden brown, about 5-7 minutes.

Push the mushrooms to the side of the skillet and add the diced chicken breasts to the pan. Cook until the chicken is browned on all sides, about 5 minutes.

Sprinkle the flour over the chicken and mushrooms, and stir well to coat everything evenly.

Gradually pour in the chicken broth, stirring constantly to prevent lumps from forming. Bring to a simmer and cook until the sauce thickens, about 3-5 minutes.

Stir in the heavy cream and dried thyme. Season with salt and pepper to taste.

Let the mixture simmer gently for another 5 minutes, or until the chicken is cooked through and the sauce has thickened.

Remove the skillet from the heat and stir in the chopped fresh parsley.

Transfer the chicken and mushroom mixture to a baking dish or individual ramekins.

Roll out the puff pastry on a lightly floured surface to fit the size of your baking dish or ramekins. Place the pastry over the filling, pressing down the edges to seal.

Use a sharp knife to make a few small slits in the pastry to allow steam to escape during baking.

Brush the pastry with beaten egg to give it a golden finish.

Place the baking dish or ramekins on a baking sheet (to catch any drips) and bake in the preheated oven for 25-30 minutes, or until the pastry is puffed and golden brown.

Remove from the oven and let the pie cool for a few minutes before serving.

Serve your delicious chicken and mushroom pie hot, with your favorite sides such as mashed potatoes and steamed vegetables. Enjoy!

Jacket Potato with Various Toppings

Ingredients:

For the jacket potatoes:

- 4 large baking potatoes
- Olive oil
- Salt

For the toppings:

- Grated cheddar cheese
- Sour cream
- Crispy bacon bits
- Chopped chives or green onions
- Butter
- Cooked chili con carne
- Guacamole
- Salsa
- Steamed broccoli florets
- Cooked and seasoned ground beef or turkey
- Sauteed mushrooms

- Caramelized onions
- Tuna salad (mixed with mayonnaise, chopped celery, and onion)
- Baked beans
- Corn kernels
- Coleslaw

Instructions:

Prepare the jacket potatoes:
- Preheat your oven to 400°F (200°C).
- Scrub the potatoes clean under running water and pat them dry with paper towels.
- Prick each potato several times with a fork to allow steam to escape during baking.
- Rub the potatoes all over with olive oil and sprinkle with salt.
- Place the potatoes directly on the oven rack or on a baking sheet lined with foil.
- Bake for 45 minutes to 1 hour, or until the potatoes are tender when pierced with a fork and the skins are crispy.

Prepare the toppings:
- While the potatoes are baking, prepare your desired toppings.
- Cook any meats, such as bacon bits or ground beef, and season them according to your preference.
- Chop any fresh ingredients, such as chives, green onions, or broccoli florets.
- Heat up any canned toppings, such as baked beans or chili con carne.

Assemble the jacket potatoes:
- Once the potatoes are baked, remove them from the oven and let them cool slightly.
- Use a sharp knife to cut a slit lengthwise across the top of each potato, being careful not to cut all the way through.
- Use a fork to fluff up the insides of the potatoes.
- Fill each potato with your desired toppings. You can mix and match different toppings to create a variety of flavor combinations.
- Serve the jacket potatoes hot, with extra toppings on the side if desired.

Enjoy:

- Serve your loaded jacket potatoes as a satisfying meal or side dish. They're perfect for lunch, dinner, or even as a party appetizer.

Feel free to get creative and experiment with different toppings to suit your taste preferences. Enjoy your delicious jacket potatoes with various toppings!

Cheese and Onion Pie

Ingredients:

For the pastry:

- 2 cups (250g) all-purpose flour
- 1/2 teaspoon salt
- 1/2 cup (115g) cold unsalted butter, diced
- 4-6 tablespoons cold water

For the filling:

- 2 large onions, thinly sliced
- 2 tablespoons butter
- 2 cups (200g) grated cheese (cheddar or your choice)
- 2 eggs, beaten
- 1/2 cup (120ml) heavy cream or milk

- Salt and pepper, to taste
- Optional: chopped fresh herbs like parsley or thyme

Instructions:

1. Prepare the pastry:

    In a large mixing bowl, combine the flour and salt. Add the cold diced butter. Using your fingertips or a pastry cutter, rub the butter into the flour until the mixture resembles breadcrumbs.
    Gradually add cold water, a tablespoon at a time, mixing until the dough comes together.
    Shape the dough into a ball, wrap it in plastic wrap, and refrigerate for at least 30 minutes.

2. Make the filling:

    In a skillet, melt the butter over medium heat. Add the thinly sliced onions and cook gently until softened and caramelized, about 15-20 minutes. Stir occasionally to prevent burning. Let them cool slightly.
    In a mixing bowl, combine the grated cheese, beaten eggs, heavy cream or milk, salt, pepper, and optional chopped herbs.
    Add the caramelized onions to the cheese mixture and stir until well combined.

3. Assemble the pie:

    Preheat your oven to 375°F (190°C).
    Roll out the pastry dough on a lightly floured surface to fit your pie dish.
    Line the pie dish with the rolled-out pastry dough, leaving any excess hanging over the edges.
    Pour the cheese and onion filling into the pastry-lined dish, spreading it out evenly.
    Fold over any excess pastry to create a rustic border, or use it to make a lattice or other decorative topping.
    Brush the pastry with a little beaten egg for a golden finish (optional).

4. Bake the pie:

   Place the pie in the preheated oven and bake for 30-35 minutes, or until the pastry is golden brown and the filling is set.
   If the pastry starts to brown too quickly, cover the pie loosely with aluminum foil.
   Once baked, remove the pie from the oven and let it cool for a few minutes before slicing and serving.

5. Serve and enjoy:

   Serve the cheese and onion pie warm, either as a main dish or as part of a meal with your favorite sides.
   This pie is delicious served with a side salad or some steamed vegetables.
   Enjoy the cheesy, savory goodness!

Feel free to customize this recipe by adding other ingredients like cooked bacon, mushrooms, or spinach to the filling, or by using different types of cheese.

Cheese Platter with Pickles

Ingredients:

For the cheese platter:

- Assorted cheeses (such as cheddar, brie, blue cheese, gouda, goat cheese, and/or aged cheeses)
- Crackers or bread slices
- Fresh fruits (such as grapes, sliced apples, or pears)
- Nuts (such as almonds, walnuts, or pecans)
- Honey or fruit preserves (optional)
- Fresh herbs (such as rosemary or thyme, for garnish)

For the pickles:

- Assorted pickled vegetables (such as cornichons, gherkins, pickled onions, pickled carrots, pickled beets, and/or pickled peppers)
- Pickled olives (such as Kalamata or green olives)

Instructions:

1. Select your cheeses:

- Choose a variety of cheeses with different textures and flavors to create a well-rounded cheese platter. Consider including a mix of soft, semi-soft, hard, and blue cheeses.

2. Arrange the cheeses:

- Place the cheeses on a large serving platter or wooden board, leaving space between each cheese for accompaniments.
- If using a soft cheese like brie or goat cheese, consider serving it in its original packaging or on a small cheese board to prevent it from spreading.

3. Prepare the accompaniments:

- Arrange crackers or bread slices around the cheeses for serving.
- Place fresh fruits such as grapes, sliced apples, or pears on the platter for a sweet contrast to the cheeses.
- Scatter nuts such as almonds, walnuts, or pecans around the platter for added texture and crunch.
- If desired, drizzle honey over some of the cheeses or serve fruit preserves on the side for a touch of sweetness.

4. Add the pickles:

- Arrange assorted pickled vegetables, such as cornichons, gherkins, pickled onions, pickled carrots, pickled beets, and pickled peppers, on the platter alongside the cheeses.
- Include pickled olives, such as Kalamata or green olives, for additional variety.

5. Garnish and serve:

- Garnish the cheese platter with fresh herbs, such as rosemary or thyme, for added color and flavor.
- Serve the cheese platter with small serving utensils for guests to help themselves.
- Encourage guests to mix and match cheeses with pickles and other accompaniments to create their own flavor combinations.

6. Enjoy:

- Enjoy your cheese platter with pickles as a delicious appetizer, snack, or party platter. Serve with wine, beer, or your favorite beverages for a complete tasting experience.

Feel free to customize your cheese platter with pickles based on your preferences and the cheeses and pickled vegetables available to you. Enjoy the delicious combination of flavors and textures!

Plaice with Tartar Sauce

Ingredients:

For the plaice:

- 4 plaice fillets

- Salt and pepper, to taste
- 1/4 cup (30g) all-purpose flour
- 2 tablespoons vegetable oil or butter
- Lemon wedges, for serving

For the tartar sauce:

- 1/2 cup (120g) mayonnaise
- 2 tablespoons chopped pickles or gherkins
- 1 tablespoon capers, chopped
- 1 tablespoon fresh parsley, chopped
- 1 tablespoon fresh lemon juice
- 1 teaspoon Dijon mustard
- Salt and pepper, to taste

Instructions:

1. Prepare the tartar sauce:

   In a small bowl, combine the mayonnaise, chopped pickles, chopped capers, chopped parsley, lemon juice, and Dijon mustard.
   Season the tartar sauce with salt and pepper to taste. Adjust the ingredients according to your preference. Cover and refrigerate until ready to serve.

2. Cook the plaice:

   Pat the plaice fillets dry with paper towels and season them with salt and pepper. Place the flour on a plate and dredge each plaice fillet in the flour, shaking off any excess.
   In a large skillet, heat the vegetable oil or butter over medium-high heat.
   Add the plaice fillets to the skillet and cook for 3-4 minutes on each side, or until they are golden brown and cooked through. The flesh should be opaque and flake easily with a fork.

3. Serve the plaice:

Transfer the cooked plaice fillets to serving plates.
Serve the plaice hot, garnished with lemon wedges and accompanied by the prepared tartar sauce.

4. Enjoy:

Serve the plaice with tartar sauce as a main dish, accompanied by your favorite side dishes such as roasted vegetables, mashed potatoes, or a fresh salad. Drizzle the tartar sauce over the plaice fillets or serve it on the side for dipping. Enjoy the delicious flavors of the tender plaice with the tangy and creamy tartar sauce.

Feel free to customize the tartar sauce according to your taste preferences by adding ingredients like chopped onions, garlic, or fresh herbs. Enjoy your plaice with tartar sauce!

Mince and Onion Pie

Ingredients:

For the filling:

- 1 lb (450g) ground beef (mince)
- 2 onions, finely chopped
- 2 cloves garlic, minced
- 1 tablespoon vegetable oil
- 2 tablespoons all-purpose flour
- 1 cup (240ml) beef stock
- 1 tablespoon Worcestershire sauce
- Salt and pepper, to taste
- Optional: chopped fresh herbs such as thyme or parsley

For the pastry:

- 2 sheets of ready-made shortcrust pastry (or homemade if preferred)
- 1 egg, beaten (for egg wash)

Instructions:

1. Prepare the filling:

    In a large skillet or frying pan, heat the vegetable oil over medium heat. Add the chopped onions and minced garlic, and cook until softened, about 5 minutes.
    Add the ground beef to the skillet and cook until browned, breaking it up with a spoon as it cooks.
    Sprinkle the flour over the beef mixture and stir well to combine. Cook for another minute to cook out the raw flour taste.
    Gradually pour in the beef stock, stirring constantly to prevent lumps from forming.
    Add the Worcestershire sauce and season with salt and pepper to taste. Stir in the optional chopped fresh herbs.
    Let the mixture simmer gently for about 10-15 minutes, or until the liquid has thickened and the flavors have melded together. Remove from heat and let it cool slightly.

2. Preheat the oven:

Preheat your oven to 400°F (200°C).

3. Assemble the pie:

    Roll out one sheet of the shortcrust pastry on a lightly floured surface to fit the bottom of a pie dish. Line the pie dish with the pastry.
    Pour the cooled mince and onion filling into the pastry-lined pie dish, spreading it out evenly.
    Roll out the second sheet of pastry to fit the top of the pie. Place it over the filling and press the edges to seal. Trim any excess pastry and crimp the edges with a fork or your fingers to create a decorative edge.
    Use a sharp knife to make a few small slits in the pastry to allow steam to escape during baking.
    Brush the top of the pastry with beaten egg to give it a golden finish.

4. Bake the pie:

    Place the pie dish on a baking sheet (to catch any drips) and transfer it to the preheated oven.
    Bake for 30-35 minutes, or until the pastry is golden brown and cooked through.

5. Serve and enjoy:

    Remove the mince and onion pie from the oven and let it cool for a few minutes before slicing.
    Serve the pie hot, accompanied by your favorite side dishes such as mashed potatoes, peas, or gravy.
    Enjoy the delicious and comforting flavors of this classic mince and onion pie!

Feel free to customize this recipe by adding other ingredients such as vegetables or herbs to the filling, or by using puff pastry instead of shortcrust pastry for the crust.

Enjoy!

Chicken Liver Pâté

Ingredients:

- 1 lb (450g) chicken livers, trimmed and cleaned
- 1 medium onion, finely chopped
- 2 cloves garlic, minced
- 4 tablespoons butter
- 1/4 cup (60ml) brandy or cognac (optional)
- 1/2 teaspoon dried thyme
- 1/2 teaspoon dried sage
- 1/4 teaspoon ground nutmeg
- Salt and pepper, to taste
- 1/2 cup (120ml) heavy cream

Instructions:

In a skillet, melt 2 tablespoons of butter over medium heat. Add the chopped onions and minced garlic, and sauté until softened and translucent, about 5-7 minutes.

Increase the heat to medium-high and add the chicken livers to the skillet. Cook the livers until they are browned on the outside but still slightly pink on the inside, about 3-4 minutes per side. Be careful not to overcook them, as they can become tough.

If using brandy or cognac, carefully pour it into the skillet and let it simmer for a minute to deglaze the pan and cook off the alcohol. Use a spatula to scrape up any browned bits from the bottom of the pan.

Season the chicken livers with dried thyme, dried sage, ground nutmeg, salt, and pepper. Stir to combine and cook for another minute to let the flavors meld.

Remove the skillet from the heat and let the mixture cool slightly.

Transfer the cooked chicken livers, onions, and garlic to a food processor or blender. Add the remaining 2 tablespoons of butter and heavy cream.

Blend the mixture until smooth and creamy, scraping down the sides of the bowl as needed. If the pâté is too thick, you can add more cream or butter to achieve your desired consistency.

Taste the pâté and adjust the seasoning with salt and pepper if needed. You can also adjust the flavors by adding more herbs or spices to taste.

Once the pâté is smooth and well seasoned, transfer it to a serving dish or ramekins.

Cover the pâté with plastic wrap, pressing it directly onto the surface to prevent a skin from forming. Refrigerate for at least 2 hours, or until firm.

Before serving, let the pâté sit at room temperature for about 15-20 minutes to soften slightly. Garnish with fresh herbs, such as parsley or thyme, if desired.

Serve the chicken liver pâté with toasted bread or crackers, cornichons, and your favorite condiments, such as mustard or fruit preserves.

Enjoy your homemade chicken liver pâté as a delicious appetizer or snack!

Salmon Fishcakes

Ingredients:

- 1 lb (450g) boneless, skinless salmon fillets
- 2 cups mashed potatoes (about 2-3 medium potatoes)
- 1/2 cup breadcrumbs (plus extra for coating)
- 2 green onions, finely chopped
- 1 tablespoon fresh dill, chopped (or 1 teaspoon dried dill)
- 1 tablespoon lemon juice
- 1 teaspoon Dijon mustard
- Salt and pepper, to taste
- 1 egg, beaten
- Vegetable oil, for frying

Instructions:

Cook the salmon:
- Preheat your oven to 375°F (190°C).
- Place the salmon fillets on a baking sheet lined with parchment paper. Season with salt and pepper.
- Bake in the preheated oven for 12-15 minutes, or until the salmon is cooked through and flakes easily with a fork. Remove from the oven and let it cool slightly.
- Once cooled, flake the salmon into small pieces using a fork.

Prepare the fishcake mixture:
- In a large mixing bowl, combine the flaked salmon, mashed potatoes, breadcrumbs, chopped green onions, chopped dill, lemon juice, Dijon mustard, salt, and pepper. Mix well to combine.
- Taste the mixture and adjust the seasoning if needed.

Shape the fishcakes:

- Divide the mixture into equal portions and shape each portion into a patty or ball. If the mixture is too sticky, you can lightly coat your hands with flour.
- Dip each fishcake into the beaten egg, then coat it with breadcrumbs, shaking off any excess.

Cook the fishcakes:
- Heat vegetable oil in a large skillet over medium heat.
- Carefully place the fishcakes in the hot oil and cook for 3-4 minutes on each side, or until golden brown and crispy.
- Remove the fishcakes from the skillet and place them on a plate lined with paper towels to drain any excess oil.

Serve:
- Serve the salmon fishcakes hot, garnished with fresh dill or lemon wedges, if desired.
- Enjoy your delicious salmon fishcakes with tartar sauce, aioli, or a squeeze of lemon juice.

These salmon fishcakes are crispy on the outside, tender and flavorful on the inside, and sure to be a hit with family and friends!

Vegetable Soup

Ingredients:

- 2 tablespoons olive oil
- 1 onion, chopped
- 2 cloves garlic, minced
- 2 carrots, peeled and diced
- 2 celery stalks, diced
- 1 bell pepper, diced
- 1 zucchini, diced
- 1 cup green beans, trimmed and cut into bite-sized pieces
- 1 can (14 oz) diced tomatoes
- 6 cups vegetable broth or water
- 1 teaspoon dried thyme
- 1 teaspoon dried oregano
- Salt and pepper, to taste
- Fresh parsley or basil, chopped (for garnish, optional)

Instructions:

Heat the olive oil in a large pot or Dutch oven over medium heat. Add the chopped onion and minced garlic, and cook until softened and fragrant, about 5 minutes.

Add the diced carrots, celery, bell pepper, zucchini, and green beans to the pot. Cook for another 5 minutes, stirring occasionally.

Pour in the diced tomatoes (with their juices) and vegetable broth or water. Stir in the dried thyme and oregano. Season with salt and pepper to taste.

Bring the soup to a boil, then reduce the heat to low. Cover and simmer for 20-25 minutes, or until the vegetables are tender.

Taste the soup and adjust the seasoning if needed. If you prefer a thicker soup, you can use an immersion blender to partially blend the soup, or simply mash some of the vegetables with a fork.

Serve the vegetable soup hot, garnished with chopped fresh parsley or basil if desired.

Enjoy your delicious and comforting vegetable soup as a nutritious meal on its own, or serve it with crusty bread or a side salad for a complete meal.

Feel free to customize this vegetable soup recipe by adding other vegetables such as potatoes, corn, spinach, or kale, or by using your favorite herbs and spices. It's a versatile dish that's perfect for using up any vegetables you have on hand. Enjoy!

Welsh Cawl

Ingredients:

- 1 lb (450g) lamb shoulder or beef stew meat, cubed
- 2 tablespoons vegetable oil
- 1 onion, chopped
- 2 cloves garlic, minced
- 2 carrots, peeled and diced
- 2 parsnips, peeled and diced
- 2 potatoes, peeled and diced
- 1 leek, trimmed, washed, and sliced
- 4 cups (about 1 liter) beef or vegetable broth
- 2 bay leaves
- 1 teaspoon dried thyme
- Salt and pepper, to taste
- Chopped fresh parsley, for garnish (optional)

Instructions:

Heat the vegetable oil in a large pot or Dutch oven over medium-high heat. Add the cubed lamb or beef and cook until browned on all sides. Remove the meat from the pot and set aside.

In the same pot, add the chopped onion and minced garlic. Cook until softened and translucent, about 5 minutes.

Return the browned meat to the pot. Add the diced carrots, parsnips, potatoes, and sliced leek.

Pour in the beef or vegetable broth, enough to cover the ingredients in the pot. Add the bay leaves and dried thyme. Season with salt and pepper to taste.

Bring the mixture to a boil, then reduce the heat to low. Cover and simmer for about 1 to 1.5 hours, or until the meat is tender and the vegetables are cooked through.

Taste the Welsh Cawl and adjust the seasoning if needed. If you prefer a thicker consistency, you can mash some of the vegetables with a fork or potato masher.

Serve the Welsh Cawl hot, garnished with chopped fresh parsley if desired. Enjoy with crusty bread or Welsh cakes on the side.

Store any leftovers in the refrigerator for up to 3-4 days. The flavors will continue to develop over time.

This Welsh Cawl recipe is perfect for a cozy dinner on a cold day or to celebrate Welsh culinary traditions. Enjoy!

Beef and Guinness Stew

Ingredients:

- 2 pounds (about 900g) beef chuck or stewing beef, cut into chunks
- Salt and pepper, to taste
- 2 tablespoons all-purpose flour
- 2 tablespoons vegetable oil
- 2 onions, chopped
- 3 cloves garlic, minced
- 2 carrots, peeled and diced
- 2 celery stalks, diced
- 2 tablespoons tomato paste
- 1 can (14.9 oz/440ml) Guinness stout beer

- 2 cups (480ml) beef broth
- 2 bay leaves
- 1 teaspoon dried thyme
- 1 teaspoon dried rosemary
- 2 tablespoons Worcestershire sauce
- 2 cups (about 300g) potatoes, peeled and diced
- Chopped fresh parsley, for garnish (optional)

Instructions:

Season the beef chunks with salt and pepper, then toss them with flour until evenly coated.

Heat the vegetable oil in a large pot or Dutch oven over medium-high heat. Add the beef in batches and brown it on all sides. Don't overcrowd the pot, as this will prevent proper browning. Remove the browned beef and set it aside.

In the same pot, add the chopped onions and cook until softened, about 5-7 minutes. Add the minced garlic, diced carrots, and diced celery, and cook for another 2-3 minutes.

Stir in the tomato paste and cook for another 2 minutes, stirring constantly.

Return the browned beef to the pot. Pour in the Guinness beer and beef broth, scraping the bottom of the pot to loosen any browned bits.

Add the bay leaves, dried thyme, dried rosemary, and Worcestershire sauce to the pot. Bring the stew to a simmer, then reduce the heat to low. Cover and let it simmer gently for about 1.5 to 2 hours, or until the beef is tender.

Add the diced potatoes to the stew and continue to simmer, uncovered, for another 30 minutes, or until the potatoes are cooked through and the stew has thickened slightly. If the stew becomes too thick, you can add more beef broth or water to reach your desired consistency.

Taste the stew and adjust the seasoning with salt and pepper, if needed.

Once the stew is ready, remove the bay leaves.

Serve the beef and Guinness stew hot, garnished with chopped fresh parsley if desired. It pairs well with crusty bread or mashed potatoes.

Enjoy your hearty and flavorful beef and Guinness stew!

Rarebit Muffins

Ingredients:

For the muffins:

- 2 cups (250g) all-purpose flour
- 1 tablespoon baking powder

- 1/2 teaspoon salt
- 1/4 teaspoon cayenne pepper (optional)
- 1/4 cup (55g) unsalted butter, melted and cooled
- 1 cup (240ml) milk
- 1 large egg

For the rarebit topping:

- 2 tablespoons unsalted butter
- 2 tablespoons all-purpose flour
- 1 cup (240ml) milk
- 2 cups (200g) grated sharp cheddar cheese
- 1 tablespoon Worcestershire sauce
- 1 teaspoon Dijon mustard
- 1/2 teaspoon paprika
- Salt and pepper, to taste
- Chopped fresh parsley, for garnish (optional)

Instructions:

1. Preheat the oven and prepare the muffin tin:

   - Preheat your oven to 375°F (190°C). Grease a 12-cup muffin tin or line it with paper liners.

2. Make the muffin batter:

   - In a large mixing bowl, whisk together the flour, baking powder, salt, and cayenne pepper (if using).
   - In a separate bowl, whisk together the melted butter, milk, and egg until well combined.
   - Pour the wet ingredients into the dry ingredients and stir until just combined. Be careful not to overmix; the batter should be slightly lumpy.

3. Fill the muffin tin:

- Divide the muffin batter evenly among the prepared muffin cups, filling each about two-thirds full.

4. Bake the muffins:

    - Place the muffin tin in the preheated oven and bake for 15-18 minutes, or until the muffins are golden brown and a toothpick inserted into the center comes out clean.
    - Remove the muffins from the oven and let them cool in the tin for a few minutes before transferring them to a wire rack to cool completely.

5. Make the rarebit topping:

    - In a small saucepan, melt the butter over medium heat. Add the flour and whisk constantly for 1-2 minutes to cook the flour and form a roux.
    - Gradually pour in the milk, whisking constantly to prevent lumps from forming.
    - Cook the sauce, stirring constantly, until it thickens and coats the back of a spoon, about 3-5 minutes.
    - Reduce the heat to low and stir in the grated cheddar cheese, Worcestershire sauce, Dijon mustard, paprika, salt, and pepper. Continue to cook and stir until the cheese is melted and the sauce is smooth and creamy.

6. Assemble the rarebit muffins:

    - Preheat the broiler in your oven.
    - Spoon a generous amount of the rarebit sauce over the tops of the cooled muffins, spreading it out evenly.
    - Place the muffins under the broiler for 1-2 minutes, or until the rarebit topping is bubbly and lightly golden brown.

7. Garnish and serve:

    - Remove the rarebit muffins from the oven and let them cool slightly.
    - Garnish with chopped fresh parsley, if desired, and serve warm.

Enjoy your delicious rarebit muffins as a savory snack or appetizer! They're perfect for any occasion and are sure to be a hit with cheese lovers.

www.ingramcontent.com/pod-product-compliance
Lightning Source LLC
LaVergne TN
LVHW081559060526
838201LV00054B/1978